Table

CW01461146

Living In the Shadow

Understanding The Narcissist and Their Weapons

Irwin Pendleton
Kindle Publishing

Kindle Direct Publishing

United States

ISBN 979-8-227-64546-3

This book is dedicated to everyone who has endured an abusive or toxic relationship and found the strength to move forward and survive.

Preface

Living in the Shadow: Understanding the Narcissist and Their Weapons offers a profound look into the intricate and often devastating tactics used by narcissistic or toxic individuals within relationships. As a credible and experienced messenger, I aim to shed light on the subtle yet calculated ways these individuals operate, manipulate, and exert control over their victims. Narcissist or toxic individuals don't just rely on a single method of control—they adapt their strategies based on the needs of the moment, the vulnerabilities of their target, and the particular type of supply they seek.

One of the key insights the book provides is how narcissists or toxic individuals select their supply. Supply, in the context of narcissism, refers to the attention, validation, and power that the narcissist craves to maintain their inflated sense of self. This supply can come in various forms—emotional, financial, or even social—and is the lifeblood of the narcissist's existence. The tactics they employ to secure and maintain this supply are as varied as the individuals they target, but they all serve one purpose: to keep the narcissist at the center of attention and in control of the relationship.

The weapons a narcissist or toxic individual uses are not always obvious. They range from emotional manipulation, gaslighting, and triangulation to more covert tactics like feigned vulnerability or playing the victim. These tools are chosen based on the needs of the narcissist or toxic individual at any given moment. If they are hunting for new supply, they may deploy charm, charisma, and flattery to lure their next target. They become everything the new person wants them to be, molding themselves into the perfect partner, friend, or confidant—all while hiding their true intentions.

However, once the narcissist or toxic individual has secured their supply, their tactics shift. The same charm and affection they used to draw the person in are replaced with subtle manipulation, criticism, and control. They weaponize their partner's insecurities, using them to create doubt and confusion. The once kind and attentive individual become cold, distant, or even cruel, but only when it serves their purpose. This constant shifting between affection and hostility is part of the narcissist's strategy to keep their supply off-balance, constantly seeking approval and validation, never knowing what to expect.

One of the most insidious weapons in the narcissist's arsenal is gaslighting. Through this tactic, the narcissist systematically erodes their victim's sense of reality. They distort the truth, deny things they've said or done, and manipulate situations to make their partner question their own memory, perception, and sanity. Over time, the victim may begin to doubt their own thoughts, becoming increasingly dependent on the narcissist or toxic individual for validation and clarity. This dependency is exactly what the narcissist or toxic individual wants—they thrive on being the one in control, the one who defines what is true and what is false.

Another powerful weapon narcissistic or toxic individual use is triangulation. This involves pitting people against one another, often by introducing a third party into the dynamic—whether it's a friend, family member, or even a romantic rival. By creating jealousy, insecurity, and competition, the narcissist ensures that their supply remains anxious and eager to win back their favor. Triangulation serves to further isolate the victim, making them feel as though they are constantly competing for the narcissist's attention and approval.

But perhaps the most deceptive weapon of all is the narcissist's ability to play the victim. When confronted or called out on their behavior, a narcissist will often turn the situation around, positioning themselves as the wronged party. They will cry, plead, and manipulate those around them into believing they are the one who has been mistreated. This tactic not only deflects blame but also garners sympathy from others, allowing the narcissist to maintain their control while discrediting anyone who dares to challenge them.

In *Living in the Shadow: Understanding the Narcissist and Their Weapons,* I delve deeply into these tactics and more, providing a roadmap for recognizing the signs of narcissistic abuse and understanding the complex dynamics at play in these toxic relationships. The narcissist or toxic individual strategies are constantly evolving, always tailored to their current needs and the vulnerabilities of their target. Whether they are seeking a new source of supply or working to maintain control over an existing one, their methods are always self-serving and destructive.

The book doesn't just expose the narcissist's weapons; it empowers readers to protect themselves. By shedding light on these behaviors, I aim to help others see through the charm, manipulation, and deceit that often defines these relationships. Awareness is the first step toward breaking free from the narcissist's grip. Once you understand the tactics they use and why they use them, you can begin to reclaim your power, set boundaries, and protect your mental and emotional well-being.

Narcissistic or toxic individuals are adept at wearing masks and concealing their true intentions, but the more you understand their tactics, the easier it becomes to see through the facade. Whether you're in a relationship with a narcissist or have been affected by one in the past, *Living in the Shadow* offers the tools and insights needed to recognize their weapons and, most importantly, to heal from the damage they've caused. By shining a light on the dark and manipulative world of narcissistic abuse, the book aims to provide not just understanding, but also hope for those seeking to break free and live authentically again.

Acknowledgments

I would like to express my deepest gratitude to everyone who purchased my work and supported me throughout this journey. Your encouragement and belief in my craft have been the driving force behind my continued passion for writing. Each of you has played a vital role in motivating me to push forward, and for that, I am truly thankful.

Without your support, this dream would not have become a reality. Every time you've shared a kind word, recommended my book to someone else, or even taken a moment to reflect on its message, you've fueled my dedication to create something meaningful. This journey is not one I could have walked alone, and your contribution to its success means more than words can express.

As I continue to grow as a writer, I hope to keep inspiring you as much as you've inspired me. This is just the beginning of what I hope will be a long and fulfilling journey. Here's to the ongoing adventure of growth, creativity, and connection. Thank you for being part of this experience with me—I couldn't have done it without you.

Prologue/Introduction

Living in the Shadow: Understanding the Narcissist and Their Weapons offers a profound look into the intricate and often devastating tactics used by narcissistic or toxic individuals within relationships. As a credible and experienced messenger, I aim to shed light on the subtle yet calculated ways these individuals operate, manipulate, and exert control over their victims. Narcissist or toxic individuals don't just rely on a single method of control—they adapt their strategies based on the needs of the moment, the vulnerabilities of their target, and the particular type of supply they seek.

One of the key insights the book provides is how narcissists or toxic individuals select their supply. Supply, in the context of narcissism, refers to the attention, validation, and power that the narcissist craves to maintain their inflated sense of self. This supply can come in various forms—emotional, financial, or even social—and is the lifeblood of the narcissist's existence. The tactics they employ to secure and maintain this supply are as varied as the individuals they target, but they all serve one purpose: to keep the narcissist at the center of attention and in control of the relationship.

The weapons a narcissist or toxic individual uses are not always obvious. They range from emotional manipulation, gaslighting, and triangulation to more covert tactics like feigned vulnerability or playing the victim. These tools are chosen based on the needs of the narcissist or toxic individual at any given moment. If they are hunting for new supply, they may deploy charm, charisma, and flattery to lure their next target. They become everything the new person wants them to be, molding themselves into the perfect partner, friend, or confidant—all while hiding their true intentions.

However, once the narcissist or toxic individual has secured their supply, their tactics shift. The same charm and affection they used to draw the person in are replaced with subtle manipulation, criticism, and control. They weaponize their partner's insecurities, using them to create doubt and confusion. The once kind and attentive individual become cold, distant, or even cruel, but only when it serves their purpose. This constant shifting between affection and hostility is part of the narcissist's strategy to keep their supply off-balance, constantly seeking approval and validation, never knowing what to expect.

One of the most insidious weapons in the narcissist's arsenal is gaslighting. Through this tactic, the narcissist systematically erodes their victim's sense of reality. They distort the truth, deny things they've said or done, and manipulate situations to make their partner question their own memory, perception, and sanity. Over time, the victim may begin to doubt their own thoughts, becoming increasingly dependent on the narcissist or toxic individual for validation and clarity. This dependency is exactly what the narcissist or toxic individual wants—they thrive on being the one in control, the one who defines what is true and what is false.

Another powerful weapon narcissistic or toxic individual use is triangulation. This involves pitting people against one another, often by introducing a third party into the dynamic—whether it's a friend, family member, or even a romantic rival. By creating jealousy, insecurity, and competition, the narcissist ensures that their supply remains anxious and eager to win back their favor. Triangulation serves to further isolate the victim, making them feel as though they are constantly competing for the narcissist's attention and approval.

But perhaps the most deceptive weapon of all is the narcissist's ability to play the victim. When confronted or called out on their behavior, a narcissist will often turn the situation around, positioning themselves as the wronged party. They will cry, plead, and manipulate those around them into believing they are the one who has been mistreated. This tactic not only deflects blame but also garners sympathy from others, allowing the narcissist to maintain their control while discrediting anyone who dares to challenge them.

In *Living in the Shadow: Understanding the Narcissist and Their Weapons,* I delve deeply into these tactics and more, providing a roadmap for recognizing the signs of narcissistic abuse and understanding the complex dynamics at play in these toxic relationships. The narcissist or toxic individual strategies are constantly evolving, always tailored to their current needs and the vulnerabilities of their target. Whether they are seeking a new source of supply or working to maintain control over an existing one, their methods are always self-serving and destructive.

The book doesn't just expose the narcissist's weapons; it empowers readers to protect themselves. By shedding light on these behaviors, I aim to help others see through the charm, manipulation, and deceit that often defines these relationships. Awareness is the first step toward breaking free from the narcissist's grip. Once you understand the tactics they use and why they use them, you can begin to reclaim your power, set boundaries, and protect your mental and emotional well-being.

Narcissistic or toxic individuals are adept at wearing masks and concealing their true intentions, but the more you understand their tactics, the easier it becomes to see through the facade. Whether you're in a relationship with a narcissist or have been affected by one in the past, *Living in the Shadow* offers the tools and insights needed to recognize their weapons and, most importantly, to heal from the damage they've caused. By shining a light on the dark and manipulative world of narcissistic abuse, the book aims to provide not just understanding, but also hope for those seeking to break free and live authentically again.

1. Can the Blind lead the Blind

"Can the blind lead the blind?" is a profound question, especially when examined through the lens of a narcissistic or toxic relationship. In such dynamics, both individuals are often lost, albeit for different reasons. The question isn't just rhetorical—it underscores the dysfunctional dance between the narcissist or toxic person and their supply. Both are trapped in a cycle where neither truly sees the reality of the situation, yet each plays a role in perpetuating the chaos.

On one hand, the person who serves as the narcissist's supply is driven by empathy, love, and a genuine desire to nurture the relationship. They act out of a deep emotional connection, often believing that their care, patience, and understanding can somehow heal the wounds of their partner or bring balance to the relationship. They might see themselves as the light in the darkness, hoping their love will change the narcissist or toxic individual for the better. But what they don't realize is that their good intentions are being manipulated and used against them.

On the other hand, the narcissist or toxic individual operates from an entirely different motivation—validation. Their actions are not fueled by love, empathy, or a desire to connect, but by a constant hunger for attention, control, and power. To them, the relationship is not a partnership but a transaction. They give only to get, and they love only to maintain their supply. Every gesture of affection, every apology, and every promise is calculated to serve their needs. The empathy of their partner is something they exploit, twisting it into a tool to keep their victim entangled in the relationship.

This creates a dangerous illusion for both parties. The supply often believes that the narcissist or toxic person cares for them in some way, even if it's deeply flawed. They cling to the moments of affection or attention, hoping that these small gestures indicate that their partner truly loves them. But in reality, these moments are just manipulations designed to maintain control. Meanwhile, the narcissist or toxic individual believes they are in complete command of the relationship, blind to the emotional damage they are causing. They are so absorbed in their need for validation that they cannot—or will not—acknowledge the destruction they leave in their wake.

The question of "who wants to leave and who wants to stay" is a constant struggle in these relationships, and the answer is never straightforward. Often, the supply wants to stay because they are invested in the relationship emotionally. They may believe that with enough love and understanding, things will improve. They may even blame themselves for the problems, thinking that if they just try harder, the narcissist will change. This is the tragic irony of the relationship—the more the narcissist abuses, the more the supply often feels compelled to fix things.

At the same time, the narcissist wants to stay because they need their supply. The relationship is not about love for them, but about maintaining control and feeding their ego. They fear abandonment not because they are emotionally attached, but because losing their supply means losing the validation they crave. Yet even though they want to stay, they continually push their partner away through manipulation, abuse, and neglect, creating a toxic push-and-pull dynamic where no one is ever truly happy.

And then, there's the constant undercurrent of loss and destruction. While both parties may have their reasons for staying, no one is truly winning in this scenario. The supply becomes emotionally, mentally, and often physically drained, giving everything without receiving anything of substance in return. They slowly lose their sense of self, becoming a shadow of who they once were, constantly questioning their worth and sanity. Meanwhile, the narcissist or toxic individual remains trapped in their cycle of manipulation and validation-seeking, never experiencing real intimacy, growth, or connection.

It's a relationship built on illusions. The supply believes in a love that doesn't truly exist, and the narcissist believes in a control that is ultimately hollow. Both are blind in their own way—the supply blinded by their empathy, the narcissist or toxic individual blinded by their ego. And like two blind individuals trying to lead each other, they are bound to stumble and fall. The relationship becomes a never-ending loop of emotional highs and devastating lows, with no resolution in sight.

The only outcome, in the long run, is loss and destruction. The supply loses their identity, their self-worth, and often their ability to trust in others. The narcissist loses any chance of genuine connection, left only with an endless cycle of seeking and discarding new sources of validation. No one truly wins, and both leave the relationship damaged, although in different ways. This dynamic reveals a painful truth: without clarity, without the ability to see the situation for what it truly is, both the narcissist and their supply are trapped in a relationship destined for failure.

Neither can lead the other out of the darkness because neither fully understands the nature of the relationship. Until one or both individuals wake up to the reality of what's happening, the cycle will continue, leaving only heartbreak, confusion, and destruction in its wake.

Ultimately, the question "Can the blind lead the blind?" serves as a metaphor for the futility of trying to find resolution or growth in a toxic or narcissistic relationship. It speaks to the inherent blindness on both sides—the victim's blindness to their own worth and the narcissist's blindness to their destructive behavior. Both are lost, and unless one person finds the strength to break free, the relationship will continue to spiral into deeper levels of dysfunction and pain.

In my first book, *Living in the Shadow: Understanding Narcissistic Supply,* I delved into the concept of chaos and how it became an unintentional addiction for me. The highs and lows of the toxic relationship with BL were so intense, so unpredictable, that the constant emotional turbulence began to feel normal—necessary, even. Chaos was the fuel that kept the relationship going, but what I didn't realize at the time was how it also kept me hooked, trapped in a cycle of emotional upheaval that was impossible to escape. It was like being on a rollercoaster I never agreed to ride, yet somehow, I couldn't get off.

Looking back, I can see clearly how this chaos shaped both BL and me. For her, it was a tool—a weapon of control. She thrived on the emotional instability, knowing that each peak of affection would keep me hanging on through the inevitable valleys of pain and manipulation. I was her Grade A supply, the perfect source of validation and energy that she could draw from at any time. My reactions, my emotions, my very presence were the fuel that powered her need for dominance and attention. The more she stirred the pot, the more she created conflict, and the more she kept me engaged, whether through arguments, drama, or just outright emotional games.

For me, chaos became something I didn't just endure—it was something I unconsciously began to expect. It's strange to think about it now, but at the time, the unpredictability became a part of my life in such a profound way that I almost felt lost without it. On some level, the volatility made the moments of calm, affection, or love seem more significant, more rewarding. When things were good, it felt like a reward for surviving the storm, and when they were bad, I believed that I just had to weather it out until things got better again. But this wasn't a real relationship—it was a trap. I wasn't playing a game that I could ever win. In fact, I wasn't even invited or asked to play.

BL made sure I was always guessing, always unsure of where I stood. One moment she'd pull me in with kindness or warmth, and the next, she'd push me away with coldness or cruelty. The pattern was so erratic that I stopped questioning it and instead focused on trying to stabilize things, not realizing that stability was never in the cards. The chaos wasn't a side effect of our relationship—it was the relationship. It was what BL needed to feel in control, and it was what kept me coming back, trying to find some sense of balance in an inherently unbalanced situation.

What I failed to realize for the longest time was that chaos was BL's preferred state of being. It was how she thrived, how she manipulated every aspect of our relationship. In her world, chaos meant control. As long as I was kept off-balance, constantly reacting to her unpredictable behavior, I was under her power. And the worst part? I didn't even see it. I thought I was fighting for love, for connection, for a future together, but in reality, I was feeding into her need for dominance and validation. Every time I tried to fix things, to calm the storm, I was playing right into her hands.

It's only now, in hindsight, that I can see how foolish I was. I was trying to win a game that wasn't meant to be won. BL never wanted resolution or peace—she wanted the chase, the drama, the emotional highs and lows that kept me tethered to her. She needed the chaos because it ensured that I would never leave, that I would keep fighting, keep trying to make things right. The more I fought, the more powerful she became, and the more I lost myself in the process.

Being her Grade A supply wasn't just about being the object of her attention—it was about being the puppet in her chaotic world, a world where the rules were constantly changing, and where my role was never clear. I became addicted to trying to solve a puzzle that had no solution, and the more I tried, the more I became ensnared in her web of manipulation.

The chaos also served another purpose for BL—it distracted me from the truth. It kept me so focused on the emotional whirlwind that I didn't have time to step back and see the bigger picture. I was too busy trying to manage the day-to-day turbulence to realize that the relationship itself was inherently toxic. The highs gave me hope, and the lows kept me busy, but in the end, both were part of the same destructive cycle. And what was the effect of all this chaos on me?

It left me emotionally drained, psychologically exhausted, and constantly questioning my worth. I became so wrapped up in trying to fix things that I lost sight of who I was outside of the relationship. BL's chaos made sure that I was always reacting, always on edge, never at peace. It wasn't just the relationship that was unstable—it was my entire sense of self. I began to believe that the problems were mine to solve, that if I just worked harder, loved more, or sacrificed enough, things would eventually get better.

But that's the cruel irony of a narcissistic or toxic relationship: the more you give, the more you lose. BL didn't want resolution, and she didn't want the calm. She thrived in the disorder, and as long as I was trying to make sense of it, I was right where she wanted me—lost in the chaos, giving her everything while receiving nothing in return.

Looking back at it, I wasn't just part of the game—I was the game. And it took me a long time to realize that the only way to win was to stop playing altogether.

2. The Troubled Sea

"But the wicked are like the troubled sea, when it cannot rest,
whose waters cast up mire and dirt."
(KJV)

- Isaiah 57:20

This verse can metaphorically relate to the mind of a narcissistic or toxic individual in a relationship. Here's how:

Restlessness: Narcissists or toxic individuals often experience an internal state of turmoil and unrest. Just as the sea in this verse is constantly churning and unable to find calm, a narcissist's mind can be marked by insecurity, dissatisfaction, or an inability to find peace. This restlessness can manifest in controlling, manipulative, or volatile behavior toward their partner.

Casting Up Mire and Dirt: The "mire and dirt" represents the negative effects that come out of their turmoil. Narcissistic or toxic individuals frequently project their inner chaos onto others, casting blame, causing confusion, or stirring up emotional drama, much like the sea casting up dirt. In relationships, this can be seen in how they destabilize their partner's emotional state by constantly creating conflict, spreading lies, or manipulating situations to their advantage. What comes to mind for me is the infamous smear campaign, a favorite tactic used by narcissistic or toxic individuals. These people weaponize their very existence to systematically destroy you, often by turning those closest to you—family, friends, and even law enforcement—against you. It's a well-crafted assault on your reputation, your integrity, and ultimately, your sense of self.

In my case, it was a little bit of both: the manipulation of law enforcement and the courts, as well as an entire church that turned its back on me. It wasn't just any betrayal; it was a staged one, meticulously planned and executed to ensure I looked like the villain in a narrative I had no control over. The performance was so convincing that people who had once known me, people I considered close, began to see me as a monster. BL led the charge in this smear campaign.

For years, she crafted a story that painted her as a helpless victim. She convinced everyone—family, friends, even the church community—that she was not truly married and that she and our children were not being supported by me, their husband and father. To them, she was a woman in desperate need, struggling to get by amidst supposed abuse and neglect. The story was heartbreaking, and people rallied around her, completely blind to the reality of the situation.

They believed she was suffering abuse, that she was a victim trapped in a miserable existence. The more she played this role, the more sympathy she garnered. The narrative was so powerful that people who had known me for years believed her without question. She played her part so well that it didn't matter what I said or did. Any attempt to explain or defend myself would only serve to reinforce her narrative.

It was like walking into a room with a glaringly obvious flaw—like having a booger on your nose—and no one around you had the decency to point it out. You know something is wrong, but no one tells you. Instead, they watch, judge, and further isolate you. Every engagement I had with people who once supported me felt like walking into this kind of trap. The stage was already set, and my wife had made sure that I looked like the antagonist, the abuser, and the person everyone should pity her for enduring.

The smear campaign was so effective that, by the time I realized what was happening, the damage was done. Any reaction I had—no matter how reasonable or justified—played directly into her hands. It supported the narrative she had spent years crafting. If I expressed anger, I was labeled as abusive. If I remained silent, I was seen as indifferent. If I defended myself, I would be accused of gaslighting. There was no way to win.

The truth is, I did play the villain in her story. But it was a role I never asked for, never deserved, and never even had a script for. She, on the other hand, was the director, writer, and star of this tragic play. She set the stage, rehearsed her lines, and executed her performance with precision. Every tear she shed, every story she told, was part of a carefully constructed narrative designed to paint me as the villain. When the show was over, her reward wasn't just the sympathy and support she received from family, friends, and the church—it was the intimacy that followed. After each successful act in the campaign, she would return to me with a sense of victory, knowing she had won the audience over yet again. The manipulation, the lies, and the betrayal weren't just tools for survival; they were her way of securing her place as the victim in everyone's eyes and of reinforcing her control over the situation.

It was as if she had won an Oscar for her performance, with friends, family, and even strangers praising her bravery and strength. Meanwhile, I was left to pick up the pieces of my shattered reputation, isolated and unable to convince anyone of the truth. The emotional toll of this kind of manipulation is profound. You begin to question your own reality, wondering if somehow, in some way, you are the person they say you are. It's a form of psychological warfare, and the narcissist knows exactly how to use it to their advantage. They thrive on the chaos they create, and their ultimate goal is to make you doubt yourself, while they remain firmly in control of the narrative.

In this toxic dance, I was cast as the villain, but in reality, I was the victim. I was trapped in a web of deceit and manipulation that left me isolated, confused, and betrayed by the very people I once trusted. The smear campaign wasn't just an attack on my character; it was an assault on my very existence. And the more I tried to escape it, the deeper I became entangled in the lies.

Looking back, I see now how calculated the entire scheme was. She wasn't just trying to destroy my reputation; she was securing her position as the perpetual victim, someone who could do no wrong, while I became the scapegoat for all her problems. Every part of my life—personal, professional, spiritual—was impacted by this relentless smear campaign. But the most painful part wasn't losing the trust of others—it was losing myself. I had been so wrapped up in trying to defend myself against the lies that I lost sight of who I really was. My identity was being rewritten in the eyes of everyone around me, and I had no control over it.

In the end, I realized that this was never about me. It was about her need for control, her need to be seen as the center of attention, the victim, and the martyr. The smear campaign was just one of many tools she used to achieve that goal. And like many others who have been in narcissistic or toxic relationships, I found myself caught in the crossfire, struggling to regain my sense of self amidst the chaos.

What the smear campaign truly reveals is the narcissist's fear of exposure. They will go to any lengths to protect their carefully constructed image, even if it means destroying the lives of those around them. In my case, it wasn't just about winning sympathy or support; it was about ensuring that no one would ever see the truth of who she really was. By painting me as the villain, she protected herself from scrutiny, ensuring that her mask of innocence remained intact. Ultimately, the smear campaign is a reflection of the narcissist or toxic individual's inner turmoil. They project their insecurities, fears, and flaws onto others, creating a distorted reality that serves their needs. And while they may win the short-term battle for public opinion, the truth has a way of revealing itself over time, which is called the "Mask Always Slips." So, Pay Close Attention!

Wickedness as Disorder: The verse associates the "wicked" with this imagery of chaos. Narcissistic or toxic behavior can be viewed as a form of moral disorder, where the individual's lack of empathy and exploitation of others disrupts the harmony of the relationship, leaving behind emotional "mire" and "dirt" for their partner to deal with.

This verse, when applied to a toxic or narcissistic individual, highlights the destructive and chaotic nature of their behavior, which prevents any true peace or harmony from being sustained in the relationship.

The Bermuda Triangle

I chose to describe my conversations with BL as the Bermuda Triangle for a reason: just like the mysterious region where things go in and never come out, our interactions seemed to pull me into an emotional black hole, leaving me lost and confused, never knowing how or why things went wrong. Conversations with BL weren't just difficult—they were intentionally designed to be confusing, disorienting, and emotionally exhausting. Whenever she wanted to communicate, she would rarely come directly to me. Instead, she would use one of the children as a messenger or have someone else present during the conversation, creating a triangulated dynamic that immediately threw me off balance. Worse yet, even when we did speak, she would communicate in riddles, never giving a straightforward answer, leaving me guessing and trying to decode what she really meant.

This use of triangulation—bringing a third party into our interactions—was one of BL's most powerful tactics. It's a common weapon in the arsenal of a narcissistic or toxic individual. By involving others, whether it was our children, a friend, or a family member, she created an atmosphere of confusion and manipulation, where I could never address anything directly or find resolution. It was like being in a maze where the exit kept shifting. I was constantly on edge, trying to figure out what was real, what was manipulation, and how to navigate a situation that was always stacked against me.

The use of triangulation is not just random; it's a deliberate tactic designed to maintain control. By involving a third party, the narcissist or toxic individual ensures that you are constantly kept guessing. You never get a moment of clarity or an opportunity to confront the real issues in the relationship.

Instead, you're left to deal with the chaos they create, wondering what the other person knows, questioning your own reality, and trying to untangle the web they've spun. BL knew exactly what she was doing—by never allowing direct communication and always keeping me off-balance, she maintained the upper hand.

So, why do narcissistic or toxic individuals rely so heavily on triangulation? It all comes down to control and power. When they can't directly dominate you through manipulation, they bring others into the mix to create confusion and division. In my case, BL used our children as pawns, positioning them between us to ensure that I could never directly address her or the issues in our relationship. She knew that by placing a third party in the middle, especially someone as emotionally charged as a child, I would be less likely to push back or demand answers. It was a brilliant, if cruel, way to maintain control without having to engage in a straightforward confrontation.

Another reason triangulation is so effective is that it forces you into a position of constantly second-guessing yourself. When someone else is brought into the conversation, you're left wondering if they're getting the same version of the story as you, or if BL was telling them something completely different behind your back. This creates a sense of paranoia and uncertainty, which only serves to further undermine your confidence and keep you dependent on the narcissist or toxic individual for any semblance of stability or understanding. You start to question your own perceptions, wondering if you're the one who's overreacting or misinterpreting things, when in reality, you're being intentionally gaslit.

For BL, triangulation wasn't just about confusion—it was about isolation. By pulling others into our relationship dynamics, she effectively isolated me from the people around me. The children, who should have been a source of comfort and support, became intermediaries in a twisted game of communication. Friends and family, when involved, were never impartial—they were drawn into her web of manipulation, often unknowingly siding with her because of the carefully crafted narrative she'd presented to them. The result was that I was left feeling completely alone, even when surrounded by people.

Riddles were another tool BL used to maintain control. Rather than having honest, open conversations, she would cloak her words in ambiguity, forcing me to constantly read between the lines and interpret what she *really* meant. It was like solving a puzzle that never had a solution. Each time I thought I had figured out what she was saying or what she wanted, the meaning would shift, leaving me more confused than before. This kept me perpetually on edge, never able to relax or trust in the communication between us.

The riddle-like conversations also served another purpose: they kept me engaged in the relationship. Even though I was frustrated, confused, and emotionally drained, I remained invested because I was always trying to figure things out. It became a twisted form of emotional labor, where I was constantly working to decode her words and actions, hoping that if I just tried hard enough, I would eventually find the truth or fix the problems in our relationship. Of course, that was never going to happen—BL had no intention of being understood or working toward resolution. Her goal was to keep me chasing after clarity that would never come, ensuring that I remained dependent on her for answers that she would never fully provide.

Triangulation, riddles, and chaos all serve the same purpose: to destabilize the victim and maintain control. By keeping me constantly confused and disoriented, BL ensured that I was never in a position to confront her directly or demand accountability. I was too busy trying to navigate the emotional minefield she had laid out to see the bigger picture of how toxic and manipulative the entire relationship had become. In the end, that's what narcissists and toxic individuals rely on—keeping you so lost in the fog of their manipulation that you can't see a way out.

Exploring why this happens brings us to the core of narcissistic behavior: a deep need for control and validation. Narcissists are terrified of losing power, so they create situations where they are always in control, even if that control is based on deception and manipulation. By using triangulation and other tactics, they ensure that their supply is always confused, always off-balance, and always dependent on them for emotional stability. It's a sick game, but one they play masterfully, often leaving their victims feeling like they are the problem when, in reality, they are just caught in a web of manipulation designed to keep them trapped.

Triangulation isn't just a weapon—it's a way to create a false reality, one where the narcissist is always in control, and everyone else is a pawn in their game. For BL, it wasn't about resolving conflicts or having meaningful conversations. It was about maintaining power over me, keeping me guessing, and ensuring that I never had the clarity or confidence to break free. And as long as I was lost in the Bermuda Triangle of our conversations, I would never be able to see the truth: that the chaos was intentional, and that my only way out was to stop playing her game altogether.

In moments of reflection or when confronted with questions about why so many people fail to recognize what's happening during triangulation, the answer often seems elusive. Why is it that, even when the signs are clear, we often choose not to see the manipulation unfolding before us? It's a difficult question, one that each of us must answer in our own way, depending on the specifics of our situation. But let's try to explore that answer together, because understanding this phenomenon is crucial for healing and moving forward.

In my case, I've come to understand why I didn't see it at first. The truth is, I didn't *want* to see it. Recognizing that BL was using triangulation to manipulate and control me would have meant admitting that the foundation of our relationship was built on something toxic. It would have meant facing the painful reality that the love, trust, and connection I thought I had were illusions carefully crafted by her. And as hard as it is to admit, that's something I wasn't ready to face at the time. I was so focused on making things work, on fixing the problems, that I turned a blind eye to the manipulation happening right in front of me. *It's not that I didn't see it—it's that I couldn't bring myself to accept it.*

But I also recognize that every situation is different, and what held me back from seeing the truth might not be what's holding you back. Maybe, for you, the manipulation is more subtle, or maybe it's woven into a relationship that has lasted for years, making it harder to untangle. Perhaps the person triangulating you is someone you deeply care about—a partner, a friend, or even a family member—and confronting the reality of their manipulation feels like too big a risk. After all, seeing the truth means that something has to change, and that can be terrifying. So instead, we bury our heads in the sand, telling ourselves that things will get better, that it's not as bad as it seems, or that we're overreacting.

Triangulation, by design, is a disorienting experience. The narcissist or toxic person intentionally creates a situation where there is always someone else involved, keeping you on edge and constantly questioning your reality. They thrive on the confusion they create, knowing that as long as you're lost in the emotional fog, you won't have the clarity to see the bigger picture. In many ways, they rely on you *not* seeing it. The longer you remain unsure, the longer they maintain control. And because of this, it's all too easy for us to brush aside the manipulation, to rationalize it away, to avoid looking too closely at what's really happening.

It's important to remember that narcissistic or toxic individuals are masters of manipulation, and part of their power lies in how skillfully they can make us doubt ourselves. They know how to use triangulation to pit people against each other, to make you feel like you're overreacting, or to convince you that you're the one who is wrong or misunderstood. They may even make you feel guilty for questioning their actions or motives, further trapping you in the cycle of confusion and emotional distress.

This is why so many people in these situations choose not to see what's happening—they're being gaslit into believing that everything is fine, that the problem is theirs to fix, or that the situation isn't as serious as it seems. One thing I have above most people is that I had seventeen long years to be molded into a character that fit someone else's illusion. No therapist or college course could have ever prepared me for what I went through. This experience was a form of education that can't be found in a textbook or a lecture. People on the outside always say, "You could have left," as if walking away is just a simple decision. That's why I'm here to tell you the truth: once the hook is in, it's not as simple as waking up one morning with an epiphany, saying, "I'm good," and walking out the door never to return. It doesn't work that way. It's not a light switch you can flip. And those who do try to leave based purely on that sudden emotional impulse often return to the relationship and end up never leaving for good.

Why does this happen? In my view, it's because they're using someone else's strength and not their own. They move out of the relationship, but it's not out of their own conviction—it's based on what others tell them or expect of them. And that never works. It's one of the most famous phrases people love to throw around: "Girl, if that was me, I would've been gone." Or "Man, you should just leave. I wouldn't put up with that." Easier said than done, right? What people don't realize is that this kind of advice often comes from individuals who are stuck in their own toxic situations but are too afraid or too blind to leave. They want to give advice, but they're not living it. They're trying to project strength, but it's a strength they haven't even found in themselves.

How toxic is that? People tell you to do something they can't even do for themselves, while you're the one who's caught in the whirlwind, struggling to keep your head above water.

It's not that simple. When you're in a narcissistic or toxic relationship, it's like your mind is in a fog, and that fog doesn't lift just because someone else tells you to go. You can't see clearly because you've been conditioned, manipulated, and worn down to the point were leaving feels like the most impossible thing in the world. You begin to believe that there's no life outside of the relationship, that this is as good as it gets. And even if you do manage to leave, the pull to return can be overpowering because you've been conditioned to need their validation, their approval, and their toxic form of love.

People who say, "If that was me, I would've been gone," don't understand that leaving a toxic relationship isn't just about physical distance. It's about emotional disentanglement, and that can take years. You don't just walk out the door and leave the memories, the manipulation, and the mental scars behind. The narcissist or toxic person has embedded themselves so deeply into your psyche that walking away feels like tearing apart your very identity. Over the years, you've been molded into a version of yourself that fits their needs, their reality, their illusion. You've been worn down piece by piece, stripped of your autonomy, and it takes time—real time, real effort—to reclaim yourself and your strength.

Leaving isn't about packing your bags and driving away. It's about rebuilding your mind, your confidence, and your sense of self. And that process is so much harder than anyone on the outside could ever imagine. The world loves to judge, to say what they would do if they were in your shoes. But they're not in your shoes. They don't understand the mental prison you've been locked in, the cycle of abuse, and the way you've been manipulated to believe that this is your fault, that you deserve this, that no one else will ever love you.

The truth is, you can't leave until you find your own strength. And that strength isn't something someone else can give you, no matter how much advice they throw your way. It's something you have to discover within yourself. You have to reach that point where you're ready, not because someone told you to be, but because you've finally realized that you deserve better. And that realization can take time. It's a process of unlearning everything the narcissist or toxic individual has ingrained in you. It's about taking back your power, one small step at a time. So, when someone says, "If that was me, I would've been gone," remind yourself that they don't know your story. They haven't lived your reality.

They don't understand the hold that a narcissist or toxic individual can have over someone, how deeply they can infiltrate your mind and heart. Leaving isn't a one-time decision—it's a journey, one that requires real strength, not borrowed strength from someone else's opinion. It's about reclaiming yourself, and that's not something that happens overnight. It's a process, a long one, and one that only you can navigate when you're truly ready.

In the end, the answer to why we don't see what happens during triangulation is deeply personal. For me, it was a combination of denial and fear of facing the truth. For you, it may be something entirely different. But whatever the reason, it's important to recognize that not seeing the manipulation doesn't mean you're weak, foolish, or unworthy. It means you're human, and you're doing your best to navigate a situation designed to keep you off balance.

What matters now is that we try to find clarity together. Acknowledging that triangulation is happening is the first step in breaking free from its grip. Whether it's through self-reflection, seeking support, or simply allowing yourself to entertain the possibility that you've been manipulated, finding the courage to see the situation for what it is will help you regain control over your life.

So, let's explore the answer to this question together. While I now know why I didn't see what was happening to me, your answer may be different. But in sharing our experiences, we can learn from each other, find strength in our shared understanding, and move forward toward healing and freedom from the toxic dynamics that have held us captive for too long. Let's not just find the answer—we'll find a path out of the confusion and back to ourselves.

Imagine the sheer force of violent waves crashing against jagged rocks—unrelenting, chaotic, and destructive. That's what's happening inside the mind of a narcissist or toxic individual. The turmoil never stops; it's a constant storm of inner conflict, unchecked emotions, and a need for control.

3. Behind the Mask

Mark 5:1-13 offers profound insights into the nature of narcissistic or toxic relationships, particularly when examining the interaction between Jesus and the man possessed by demons. This passage can be interpreted symbolically to shed light on the dynamics of control, manipulation, and eventual liberation from the suffocating grip of a toxic individual. The passage recounts how Jesus encounters a man living among the tombs, possessed by a legion of demons. The man is in torment, isolated from society, and controlled by forces that dominate his mind and body. When Jesus approaches, the demons recognize His authority and plead to remain within the man, ultimately requesting to be cast into a herd of pigs instead of being sent away entirely. Jesus grants their request, and the demons enter the pigs, who then rush into the sea and drown.

Parallels to a Narcissistic or Toxic Relationship

The story of the demon-possessed man offers rich allegory for understanding the suffocating nature of a narcissistic or toxic relationship. While the passage describes spiritual possession, it mirrors the emotional and psychological "possession" experienced by individuals trapped in such relationships.

Isolation and Control

The man in the story lives among the tombs, cut off from his community and human connection. This mirrors the isolation a person in a toxic relationship often feels. A narcissist seeks to control their partner, cutting them off from their support network of family and friends, much like the demons isolate the man from society. The individual becomes trapped in the tombs of their own mind—metaphorically dead to the world around them, existing in a state of emotional paralysis, unable to escape the grasp of the controlling influence.

In a narcissistic or toxic relationship, isolation is a key tactic. The narcissist or toxic individual ensures that their partner has little to no access to outside perspectives, friends, or emotional support, making it easier to manipulate them. Just as the man's mind is consumed by the demons, a victim of narcissistic or toxic abuse often finds their thoughts dominated by the toxic partner, who creates an environment of fear, dependency, and confusion. It's the constant emotional and psychological feeling of walking on eggshells, a state of perpetual anxiety where every step, word, or action feels like it could trigger an eruption.

Imagine a child who is being abused, desperate to tell someone what's happening to them, but the moment they try, their parent makes a subtle movement—perhaps raising a hand or stepping toward them—and the child instinctively flinches, bracing for a hit. That single, automatic reaction speaks volumes about the fear and trauma they carry, yet it often goes unnoticed. This silent cry for help can persist for years, with the child constantly living in fear, yet no one steps in to stop it.

Why? Is it that no one sees the signs—the subtle flinches, the forced smiles, the tense body language—or is it that no one truly cares because the abuse isn't happening to them? Society has an alarming way of turning a blind eye to pain when it's too uncomfortable to confront, especially if it disrupts the idealized image of a perfect family or relationship. People often choose to ignore what's right in front of them, convincing themselves that it's not their place to intervene or that it can't be as bad as it seems.

In narcissist or toxic relationships, whether between a parent and child or between adults, this dynamic of fear and denial thrives. The abuser maintains power through intimidation and control, while the victim becomes conditioned to anticipate punishment even when it's not immediately clear if it's coming. That constant flinching, whether physical or emotional, is the hallmark of someone who has learned to survive in a hostile environment. They have become experts at predicting danger, even when it's masked by a smile or a kind gesture.

But what's even more tragic is the response—or lack thereof—by those who witness these signs. It's not just that people don't notice; sometimes, they simply choose not to act. Perhaps they don't want to get involved, or they rationalize the situation by assuming that someone else will step in. Maybe they convince themselves that the abuser can't really be that bad, or they focus on the abuser's charm and outwardly pleasant demeanor. After all, how could someone who seems so friendly or successful behind closed doors be capable of such cruelty?

The truth is, people often find it easier to look the other way, to maintain the illusion that everything is fine, rather than confront the uncomfortable reality of abuse. It's as though, by ignoring the problem, they can distance themselves from it, pretending it doesn't exist simply because it doesn't directly affect them. And so, the cycle continues. The victim remains trapped, flinching and bracing for harm, while those who could intervene stay silent.

This bystander apathy, whether from friends, family, or society at large, is one of the most insidious aspects of abuse. It allows the abuser to continue unchecked, while the victim is left feeling even more isolated and powerless. They start to believe that their pain doesn't matter, that no one will help them because no one cares enough to notice. The world around them becomes complicit in their suffering, not through active malice but through passive indifference.

This indifference is often driven by discomfort or fear of confrontation. People don't want to disrupt their own lives by getting involved in someone else's turmoil. They avoid the responsibility of taking action, choosing to maintain their own comfort over the well-being of the victim. But this avoidance is a form of complicity, enabling the abuse to continue unchecked. In failing to act, society effectively becomes another layer of the abuse, reinforcing the message that the victim's suffering is invisible or unimportant.

For the person (known as supply) enduring this torment, the feeling of being unheard or unnoticed only compounds their pain. They are left not only dealing with the abuse itself but also grappling with the crushing weight of knowing that those around them—those who could make a difference—are choosing to remain silent. It's a form of abandonment, a further betrayal, because what hurts even more than the abuse is the realization that no one cares enough to stop it or tries to help.

This silence allows the narcissist or toxic individual to flourish. Narcissistic or toxic individuals often manipulate not just the victim but also the perceptions of those around them. They know how to present a charming, caring, or even victimized persona to the outside world, making it difficult for others to believe the truth. This facade allows them to maintain control, while the victim remains trapped in the shadow of fear, unable to escape.

In these narcissistic and toxic environments, it's not just about the physical acts of abuse; it's about the psychological or emotional toll of never feeling safe, of always anticipating the next blow, even if it doesn't come. The constant tension, the emotional flinching, becomes a way of life. Over time, the victim becomes conditioned to accept this reality as normal, even as they desperately yearn for escape. But it doesn't have to be this way. The cycle of abuse and the complicity of silence can be broken. It starts with noticing the signs—the flinching, the withdrawal, the quiet desperation—and acting on them. It requires the courage to confront uncomfortable truths, to speak up when it would be easier to stay silent. It demands empathy, the willingness to care about someone else's pain even when it's not happening to you.

In the end, breaking the silence is the first step toward healing. For the victim/supply, it signals that they are seen, that their suffering matters, and that they are not alone. For those around them, it's a chance to be part of the solution rather than another layer of the problem. It's about choosing to care, even when it's easier not to. Because if we don't, the flinching continues, and the cycle of abuse goes on unchecked.

The Torment of the Mind

The man in Mark 5 is described as being constantly tormented, crying out and cutting himself with stones. This self-destructive behavior can be likened to the emotional and psychological harm inflicted by a toxic or narcissistic partner. In such relationships, the victim may suffer from feelings of worthlessness, anxiety, and despair, to the point where they may even begin to question their own sanity, much like the man who was controlled by forces beyond his comprehension.

A narcissist or toxic individual exerts psychological control by creating chaos, confusion, and emotional instability. Gaslighting is one tactic they use, leading the victim to doubt their own reality and sense of self. Over time, the victim becomes so consumed by the pain and confusion that they begin to lose sight of who they truly are. This emotional and mental fragmentation is much like the man being torn apart by the demons that inhabited him.

The Fear of Losing Control

When Jesus arrives, the demons immediately recognize His authority. They fear being cast out because they know they are about to lose their grip over the man they have possessed. This reflects a narcissist's fear of losing control over their partner. Narcissists rely on maintaining power, and when they sense that their control is slipping—perhaps because the victim is beginning to recognize the toxicity of the relationship—they will often panic and escalate their abusive tactics. This might include more manipulation, emotional outbursts, or attempts to regain control through guilt or fear.

In the story, the demons plead with Jesus not to send them away completely, showing their desperation to remain in power. Similarly, a narcissistic or toxic individual will often do anything to avoid losing the control they have over their partner, going to great lengths to maintain their dominance. Whether through emotional manipulation, threats, or playing the victim, the narcissist or toxic individual mirrors the demons' plea to continue their torment. Interestingly, BL repeatedly expressed confusion over why I wanted to end the relationship, almost as if she couldn't fathom a world where I would choose to walk away from her.

She seemed genuinely baffled, acting as though I could never do better without her, as if my entire existence would crumble without her presence. It was a strange mix of disbelief and arrogance, as though she truly believed that my identity, my happiness, and my success were entirely tethered to her, that I was somehow incapable of thriving without her.

Her attempts to play the victim were almost theatrical. She would feign ignorance about the divorce I filed, claiming she had no idea why it was happening, despite the fact that she was the one who signed the paperwork first. It was an incredible display of manipulation, as if rewriting history could somehow erase the fact that she had initiated key steps toward the end of the marriage. She acted like a bystander in her own life, like the consequences of her actions weren't hers to own, instead painting herself as the innocent party blindsided by events beyond her control.

But the truth was undeniable. Despite her efforts to convince me—and perhaps herself—that she was unaware of what was happening, the reality was that she had always been the architect of this narrative. From the beginning, she controlled the storyline, and now, as it all came crumbling down, she tried to erase her role in it. She wanted to cling to the power dynamic that had always worked in her favor, where she was the center and I was orbiting around her, dependent on her approval and presence to validate my worth.

Yet, her attempts to gaslight me into believing that I couldn't do better without her were just more layers of the manipulation that defined our relationship. She wanted me to doubt myself, to question my decision to break free, hoping that I would eventually come crawling back, convinced that life without her was unthinkable. This was a classic move in the narcissistic playbook: make the other person feel small, insignificant, incapable of thriving outside the toxic bubble you've created for them.

The irony was that she didn't realize how much stronger I had become, how much clarity I had gained in seeing her manipulation for what it was. It wasn't just about wanting to leave; it was about reclaiming my own sense of self, my own identity that had been smothered under years of psychological warfare. BL couldn't understand why I would want to break it off because, in her mind, she was the prize, the one holding everything together. She genuinely believed that I needed her more than she needed me.

But the truth was that, without her, I could finally breathe. Without her constant manipulation, her endless mind games, I could begin to rebuild a life that was centered on my own values, my own choices, and my own sense of self-worth. I had spent so long being made to feel like I wasn't enough, like I couldn't function without her, that when I finally made the decision to leave, it was the most liberating moment of my life.

Her denial about the divorce, despite being the first to sign the paperwork, was just another desperate attempt to maintain control over the situation. By acting as though she had no idea what was happening, she was trying to rewrite the narrative, to make herself appear innocent while I was cast as the unreasonable one. But her signature on that paper was proof that she had always known. She had always been an active participant in the unraveling of our relationship, no matter how much she tried to distance herself from the truth. BL's refusal to acknowledge the reality of our situation, her insistence that she didn't know why I wanted to end things, was a final attempt to hold on to the illusion of control. She had constructed this idea that she was indispensable, that I was somehow helpless without her. But by walking away, I shattered that illusion. I wasn't the one who was lost without her. She was the one who couldn't comprehend a life where she wasn't the center of someone else's universe.

Her confusion wasn't about not understanding why I wanted to leave; it was about not being able to accept that I could, and would, leave her behind. Her shock wasn't rooted in any genuine confusion but rather in the realization that her hold over me had finally been broken. She was no longer the puppet master pulling the strings. And for someone like BL, that loss of control was the most devastating blow of all. Walking away seems difficult, you must believe it is possible. We made ourselves believe that we could leave now change the channel and leave. Think about it **"YOU"** made yourself stay so that means **"YOU"** have the power to leave!

The Power of Liberation

Jesus, with His authority, casts the demons into a herd of pigs, who then rush into the sea and drown. This act of liberation is symbolic of breaking free from the grip of a toxic or narcissistic individual. Just as the man is freed from the demons that tormented him, a person in a toxic relationship can find liberation once they recognize the truth of the situation and take steps to break free. However, liberation from a narcissist or toxic individual is often met with resistance. Just as the demons attempt to find another host, the narcissist may try to find new ways to control or manipulate their victim, even after the relationship has ended. But just as the pigs rushed to their destruction, the narcissist's attempts to maintain control often self-destruct once the victim becomes aware of their tactics and seeks help.

The drowning of the pigs represents the final collapse of the narcissist or toxic individual power. When a person (supply) breaks free from a narcissistic or toxic relationship, the grip that once seemed so strong and unbreakable is shattered. The individual (supply) is no longer consumed by the fear, guilt, or confusion that once kept them in bondage. Much like the man who is restored to his right mind, the victim of narcissistic or toxic abuse can begin to reclaim their identity, heal from the wounds of the relationship, and re-enter society as a whole, healed person.

The Aftermath of Freedom

Once the demons are gone, the man is found sitting, clothed, and in his right mind—a stark contrast to the tormented soul he once was. This transformation is a powerful representation of what it looks like to recover from a narcissistic or toxic relationship. The journey to healing may take time, but once the hold of the narcissist or toxic individual is broken, the individual (supply) can begin the process of rebuilding their life, rediscovering their sense of self, and reconnecting with the world around them. The people in the town were astonished by the man's transformation, much like those around a victim of a narcissistic or toxic relationship might be surprised by their recovery and newfound strength.

The scars may remain, but the individual has been liberated from the force that once dominated them.

The Narcissist's Next Move

Interestingly, after the man is freed, the townspeople react with fear and ask Jesus to leave. This is reminiscent of how, in the aftermath of a toxic relationship, some people may be uncomfortable with the truth being revealed. Those who were manipulated by the narcissist may struggle to accept the reality of what happened, either out of denial or discomfort.

The narcissist or toxic individual, having lost their power, may quickly move on to find new victims, just as the demons sought new hosts. The narcissist or toxic individual's primary concern is control, and when they lose one source, they often move on to others. Just as the demons were cast out and sought another host in the pigs, a narcissist may seek a new person to dominate once their current target breaks free.

Mark 5:1-13 offers a symbolic look at the dynamics of a narcissistic or toxic relationship, highlighting the torment, control, and isolation experienced by the victim. It also offers hope by illustrating the power of liberation and healing. Just as the man was freed from the demons that controlled him, individuals in toxic relationships can find freedom through awareness, support, and a reclaiming of their identity. Breaking free from a narcissist or toxic relationship is no small feat, but the story reminds us that even the most seemingly insurmountable forces of control can be overcome. Liberation, healing, and restoration are possible, and like the man who was freed, victims of toxic relationships can reclaim their lives, find peace, and move forward in wholeness.

4. Why There Can't Be Only One

John 4:1-42, which recounts the story of Jesus' encounter with the Samaritan woman at the well, offers powerful insights into the dynamics of a narcissistic or toxic relationship when viewed through a psychological and emotional lens. This passage not only highlights themes of personal transformation and healing but also touches on deeper issues such as shame, manipulation, and the need for validation—key components that often play a role in narcissistic or toxic relationships.

Emotional Thirst and Dependency

In the story, the Samaritan woman is depicted as someone who has been in multiple relationships—having had five husbands and now living with a man who is not her husband. This history of broken relationships reflects a pattern of emotional/psychological thirst and unfulfilled needs. In many narcissistic or toxic relationships, the individual being manipulated or controlled often experiences a deep emotional and psychological void, much like the Samaritan woman. They may seek validation and fulfillment from external sources—partners, friends, or even the narcissist or toxic individual themselves—without realizing that these relationships are only deepening their sense of inadequacy.

Narcissistic or toxic relationships often create a cycle of dependency. The victim, like the Samaritan woman, is emotionally and psychologically thirsty, constantly seeking from the relationship something that will never truly satisfy them. *The narcissist or toxic individual capitalizes on this, offering just enough validation or affection to keep the person hooked, while simultaneously withholding real love or support. The emotional thirst becomes a cycle, where the person in the relationship keeps returning to the well, only to leave feeling empty once again.* – This is why one supply can never be enough for the narcissist or toxic individual.

One supply is never enough for a narcissist or toxic person because of their insatiable need for validation, control, and admiration, all driven by deep emotional and psychological deficiencies. Narcissists constantly crave validation to bolster their fragile self-esteem, which relies on external affirmation. Over time, one person, no matter how attentive, cannot provide the continuous stream of admiration they desire, leading the narcissist to seek new sources. Additionally, narcissists often become bored with familiarity; once they feel they've gained control over someone, the excitement fades, pushing them to seek fresh attention. This is further compounded by their deep fear of abandonment—relying on just one person makes them vulnerable to rejection. To mitigate this fear, they cultivate multiple sources of supply, ensuring they always have a backup to maintain their self-worth.

The need for control also drives the narcissist or toxic individual to juggle multiple relationships, as one person (source of supply) may not be enough to satisfy their dominance. *Pay Attention!* **Different individuals (supply) fulfil different roles—offering admiration, emotional support, or conflict—which provides the narcissist or toxic individual with varied forms of validation. Over time, their primary source of supply may become emotionally and psychologically drained due to their constant demands, so the** *narcissist or toxic individual begins to seek new targets to replenish their needs. This cycle of manipulation and emotional extraction is often fuelled by their addiction to the highs of admiration and drama (chaos), which one person alone cannot sustain.*

Furthermore, narcissists dehumanize others, viewing them as tools for their own gratification rather than as individuals with their own needs and feelings. This mindset makes it easy for them to discard one person and move on to another without guilt or concern for the emotional damage they cause. Ultimately, the narcissist or toxic individual unsustainable expectations and relentless pursuit of external validation create a cycle where one source of supply is never enough to satisfy their ever-growing needs for attention, control, and superiority.

Shame and Isolation

The woman's status as an outcast in her community is significant. She comes to draw water from the well at midday, a time when no one else would be around, indicating that she is avoiding others due to shame. In a narcissistic or toxic relationship, shame plays a central role. The toxic individual often manipulates their partner into feeling unworthy or ashamed, isolating them emotionally and socially. Much like the Samaritan woman, victims (supply)of narcissistic or toxic relationships may find themselves isolated from friends, family, and even their own sense of self-worth. They carry the weight of their partner's manipulation and may feel as though they cannot share their true experiences with others for fear of judgment or disbelief.

Recalling the image in the first book, where a man and a woman stood in such a way that you couldn't tell who the abuser or the victim was, I found myself deeply resonating with that confusion. BL had me so emotionally and psychologically drained that I began to believe everything that went wrong in the relationship was my fault. The lines between who was causing the harm and who was suffering from it became blurred. At times, I found myself desperate to make things right, constantly searching for ways to fix what I thought I had broken.

This experience wasn't just about emotional and psychological exhaustion; it was the gradual erosion of my sense of self. When someone manipulates you in such a way that you start questioning your reality, it becomes incredibly hard to regain a clear perspective. Over time, I internalized the blame for all the issues in the relationship, from minor disagreements to major conflicts. I was always walking on eggshells, constantly assessing my actions and their potential to upset the balance. And despite my efforts to fix things, nothing ever seemed to improve.

On one hand, this mindset made me hyper-aware of my own behavior, pushing me to reflect on how I could improve as a partner. It could be argued that such introspection can help build self-awareness and empathy. But the downside was far more destructive. It put me in a cycle of guilt and self-blame that kept me tethered to the toxic dynamic, feeding BL's need for control and preventing me from seeing her manipulation for what it was. In this constant quest to make things right, I lost sight of my own needs and boundaries, allowing the emotional abuse to continue unchecked.

The real danger of this situation is that the victim(supply) often loses the ability to see the narcissist or toxic individual tactics for what they are. When you're made to feel responsible for the relationship's dysfunction, it's hard to step back and recognize that the problem isn't entirely you. It's this very confusion—the inability to clearly identify the abuser—that makes toxic relationships so damaging. The narcissist or toxic individual thrives on ambiguity, on making their victim (supply) feel just uncertain enough to remain trapped in the cycle.

For anyone in a similar situation, it's essential to recognize that while relationships do require effort from both parties, no one should bear the full weight of responsibility, especially when manipulation and emotional/psychological abuse are at play. The challenge lies in regaining the clarity to distinguish between healthy self-reflection and toxic self-blame, something that can often only be achieved with external support or professional help. Without it, the narcissist or toxic individual will continue to exploit that confusion, feeding their narcissistic or toxic needs while the victim (supply) becomes more entangled in the false belief that they are the source of the problem.

Isolation serves the narcissist or toxic individual agenda, as it prevents the victim (supply) from seeking help or finding a way out. Just as the woman's shame led her to draw water alone, people in narcissistic or toxic relationships often withdraw from social circles and support systems, further enabling the narcissist or toxic individual control.

The Narcissist's Role: Exploiting Vulnerability

Although the passage does not present Jesus as a narcissist or toxic individual (quite the opposite/HE IS GOD), we can draw a contrast between His actions and those of a toxic or narcissistic individual. Where Jesus offers the woman true compassion and understanding, a narcissist or toxic individual would exploit her vulnerabilities for their gain. In a narcissistic or toxic relationship, the abuser seeks to control their partner by exploiting their emotional and psychological wounds, fears, and insecurities.

In the story, Jesus reveals the woman's past, not to shame her but to bring her healing and understanding. He acknowledges her history without judgment and offers her "living water," a symbol of spiritual and emotional/psychological fulfillment that transcends the superficial relationships she has been engaged in. *A narcissist or toxic individual, on the other hand, would use such knowledge as a weapon—highlighting her failures and weaknesses to manipulate and belittle her, ensuring that she remains dependent on their approval and validation.*

Manipulation and False Promises

The concept of "living water" that Jesus offers can be contrasted with the false promises often made in narcissistic or toxic relationships. A narcissist or toxic individual may lure their partner with the illusion of love, security, or happiness, but these promises are never fulfilled. The partner (supply), like the Samaritan woman, might continue returning to the "well" of the relationship, hoping to quench their emotional and psychological thirst, but always leaving unsatisfied. Narcissist or toxic individuals give just enough attention or affection to keep their partner (supply) engaged, but never enough to meet their true emotional and psychological needs.

This dynamic creates a sense of psychological and emotional exhaustion, much like the woman who comes to the well every day, only to leave with temporary relief. The victim (supply) in a narcissistic or toxic relationship is left constantly chasing something they will never truly receive—whether it's love, respect, or validation. Most in the circle of narcissistic or toxic relationships often refer to a tactic known as "Future Faking," which perfectly describes the manipulative behavior BL used to string me along. She would paint these vivid pictures of a future where everything would be better, promising that we could finally be a family, if only I did certain things.

It was like dangling a carrot in front of me—just out of reach—making me believe that if I worked a little harder or changed just a bit more, everything would magically fall into place. The idea of a happy family, of harmony, of finally being seen and appreciated, was so seductive that I kept chasing after it, hoping that the next day would be different. But it never was. The promises were just that—empty words designed to keep me on the hook.

It reminded me of a smooth-talking car salesman, pitching the deal of a lifetime. They'd say all the right things: "How fast do you want to go? This model has the latest features, and there's a special deal just for you, but it's only available today." It sounds so convincing, almost too good to be true. You're sold on the dream of what you could have, and before you know it, you're handing over everything you have, believing you're getting something worthwhile in return. But just like with those salesmen, you end up driving off with a product that never quite lives up to the promises made. That shiny exterior hides deeper issues—faults and cracks that you only discover after it's too late.

BL knew exactly how to craft these fantasies, weaving together a picture of a life that felt so close, so attainable, but just always slightly out of reach. She would say things like, "We can be a family if you only do this," or, "Things will get better once we get through this rough patch." The problem was, the "rough patch" never ended, and the goalposts were always moving. Just like the car salesman, she had a new offer, a new promise, a new future waiting just around the corner—if only I would comply. It was the ultimate manipulation, keeping me in a state of perpetual hope while never delivering on any of those promises.

The brilliance of future faking is that it taps into your deepest desires. BL knew that what I wanted more than anything was stability, a sense of belonging, a family that functioned in harmony. She used that knowledge to keep me stuck, always hinting that the life I dreamed of was just one more step away. It's a particularly cruel form of manipulation because it plays on your hope, the one thing that keeps you going even when the situation is unbearable. And hope is a powerful drug. When you believe that things "could" get better, you're willing to endure more than you ever thought possible. You tell yourself that all the pain and suffering will be worth it in the end because you believe in the fantasy, they've sold you.

But here's the thing: just like with that first car, once you're in it for a while, you start noticing the flaws. You see the wear and tear, the broken promises hidden beneath the shiny exterior. You realize that the future you were promised was never going to happen—it was all just a mirage. And by the time you come to terms with that, you've already invested so much. It's hard to admit that you've been played, that you were sold a dream that was never real. So, you keep holding on, convincing yourself that maybe if you just did "one more thing", everything would fall into place. Maybe this time, the promise will come true.

This is the cruel cycle of future faking. It keeps you tethered to a relationship that is slowly eroding your sense of self, your confidence, your very soul. You're trapped in a loop of false hope, and the narcissist or toxic individual knows exactly how to keep you there. They throw just enough breadcrumbs to make you believe that the dream is still alive, that the future you want is still possible, but it's all smoke and mirrors.

The truth is, they were never going to give you the future they promised. It was never about building a life together or creating a happy family. It was about control. By making you chase after a fantasy, they maintain their power over you. They keep you focused on what *could* be instead of what *is*. And as long as you're focused on that distant future, you're not paying attention to the damage being done in the present.

Looking back, I see how expertly BL wielded this tactic. She played on my desires, my hope, and my need for connection to keep me stuck in a relationship that was toxic and damaging. And the worst part? I bought into it. Just like the excited car buyer, I believed the pitch. I wanted to believe it. Because the alternative—the truth—was too painful to accept.

Future faking is one of the most insidious tools a narcissist or toxic individual has. It's a promise of a better tomorrow that never comes, a manipulation designed to keep you hooked and compliant. And once you recognize it for what it is, you begin to see how deeply you were manipulated, how expertly your hope was used against you. The challenge, then, is to reclaim your own future—to stop chasing the one they dangle in front of you and start building one for yourself, free from their lies and manipulation.

Self-Realization and Empowerment

A key moment in the passage is when the Samaritan woman recognizes Jesus as the Messiah. This revelation transforms her, empowering her to leave behind her past and share her experience with her community. Similarly, in a narcissistic or toxic relationship, self-realization is often the turning point for the victim (supply). Once they recognize the truth of the situation—whether it's emotional and psychological abuse, manipulation, or control—they can begin to reclaim their power and break free from the toxic dynamic.

This moment of awakening is crucial for healing. Just as the Samaritan woman goes from being an outcast to a messenger of truth, individuals in narcissistic or toxic relationships often undergo a transformation once they break free from the narcissist or toxic individual's influence. They find their voice, their sense of self, and the strength to rebuild their lives.

However, the journey to self-realization is often met with resistance from the narcissist or toxic individual, who fears losing control. In a toxic relationship, the abuser may escalate their manipulative tactics to prevent their partner from leaving, much like how the forces of darkness resist when someone seeks the light of truth. But once the victim sees the reality of the situation, much like the Samaritan woman realizing the truth about her encounter with Jesus, there is no going back. The path to healing has begun.

Breaking Free from the Past

The Samaritan woman's encounter with Jesus also symbolizes the possibility of breaking free from a painful past. She had been defined by her relationships, by the men in her life, and by the judgment of her community. In narcissistic or toxic relationships, the victim (supply) is often trapped by the narratives created by the narcissist or toxic individual—the story that they are unworthy, that they cannot survive without the abuser, that their life outside the relationship will be worse than within it. Jesus offers her a new identity, one not tied to her past or her relationships, but to something deeper and more fulfilling.

In the same way, breaking free from a narcissistic or toxic relationship involves reclaiming one's identity apart from the abuser's manipulation and control. It's about recognizing that your worth is not defined by another person's opinion of you, but by your own intrinsic value.

Healing and Wholeness

Ultimately, Jesus offers the Samaritan woman something that transcends the immediate problem of her failed relationships: He offers her spiritual and emotional/psychological healing. *For someone coming out of a narcissistic or toxic relationship, the journey is not just about leaving the abuser, but about finding inner healing and wholeness. The wounds inflicted by emotional/psychological manipulation and abuse run deep, and it takes time to rebuild one's sense of self-worth and trust in others*. Just as the woman at the well experienced a transformation through her encounter with Jesus, individuals who break free from narcissistic or toxic relationships have the opportunity for profound personal growth. The "living water" they seek may be found in self-love, in supportive relationships, or in a renewed sense of purpose and direction in life.

John 4:1-42 provides a powerful metaphor for understanding the dynamics of a narcissistic or toxic relationship. The Samaritan woman's emotional and psychological thirst, her isolation, and her eventual liberation mirror the experiences of many who have been trapped in controlling and manipulative relationships. Through self-realization, breaking free from past narratives, and seeking true healing, there is hope for recovery and renewal. The story reminds us that no matter how deep the wounds of a narcissistic or toxic relationship, transformation and healing are always possible when the truth is acknowledged and embraced. *~ The Truth Is There Is No Water in the Well, so Stop Trying to Fill Up!*

To fully grasp why one source of supply is never enough for a narcissist or toxic individual, it's important to delve deeper into the psychological mechanisms that govern their behavior. Narcissist or toxic individuals, at their core, have a distorted and fragile sense of self that is built on shaky foundations of insecurity, despite outward displays of grandiosity or confidence. The complexities of their personality make it impossible for them to rely on one person for the affirmation they crave. Their emotional and psychological void is so deep that no single individual could ever provide enough validation, control, or admiration to satisfy their unending thirst for attention.

Fragile Ego and Fear of Inadequacy

Narcissist or toxic individuals are often perceived as people who possess an inflated sense of self-importance, yet this inflated ego is a facade that hides a deep fear of inadequacy. Beneath the surface, they are terrified of being exposed as ordinary or flawed. This deep-seated fear drives them to seek constant reinforcement from multiple sources. One individual's admiration or love is fleeting in their eyes, and they feel an almost compulsive need to seek new admiration to maintain the illusion of superiority. A single person's praise quickly loses its potency because, to the narcissist or toxic individual, the closer someone gets, the more aware they become of their own perceived flaws. To avoid facing these insecurities, they seek out new people who can offer fresh praise or admiration, as it helps mask their feelings of inadequacy.

One of the core reasons they can't rely on one source of supply is that this supply inevitably sees through the mask. The closer someone gets to a narcissist or toxic individual, the more they realize that the image projected by the narcissist or toxic individual is an illusion. This realization, even if unspoken, becomes a threat to the narcissist. They can't tolerate the idea that someone might see them as anything less than perfect, so they seek out new people who haven't yet seen through their façade. This constant rotation of new sources of supply serves as a buffer against the fear of being exposed.

Avoiding Intimacy and Vulnerability

Intimacy is a threat to narcissist or toxic individual because it requires vulnerability, and vulnerability, to them, means weakness. True intimacy involves revealing one's flaws, insecurities, and fears—something a narcissist or toxic individual cannot bear to do. They thrive on superficial connections where they can control the narrative and project an image of perfection. Deep relationships, however, expose their human imperfections.

Because intimacy forces people to confront their true selves, narcissistic or toxic individuals avoid it by keeping relationships shallow. They rely on multiple sources of supply to prevent any one person from getting too close. By juggling several relationships—whether romantic, familial, or social—they avoid the risk of emotional/ psychological exposure. The more spread out their attention is, the less likely any one person can hold them accountable or force them to confront their insecurities. This brings to mind one of the most telling signs of infidelity within a relationship with a narcissistic or toxic individual: when they start weaponizing their body to control you, using intimacy—or the lack thereof—as a tool to bring you under submission. It's a slow and subtle shift at first, but soon it becomes clear that physical affection is no longer about connection or love; it's about control. Depriving you of intimacy becomes a form of punishment, a way to make you feel less worthy, and a means to maintain power over your emotional well-being.

One of their tactics is to withdraw affection under the guise of dissatisfaction, saying things like, "I don't like this or that," or "Maybe we should try something different because I'm tired of the same routine." Suddenly, you're made to feel as if you're the problem, as if you're not enough or that you're failing to meet their needs. This tactic is designed to make you jump through hoops to prove your worth and to keep you constantly trying to please them. You're left feeling like if you just make a few changes, if you become more what they want, then maybe the intimacy and affection will return. But that's part of the manipulation—because the goalposts are always moving, and no matter what you do, it will never be enough.

Then comes the "Okay." It's subtle, but that one word is enough to suck you back in, making you believe that things can change if you just comply with their demands. You fall into the trap of thinking that perhaps this time, you'll be able to fix things, that maybe if you try harder or bend to their whims, the relationship will get back on track. But what you don't realize is that this is all practice for them—for the new supply they're grooming or even the old supply they've kept hidden in the shadows. They are testing out their manipulation tactics on you, refining them, and using them to control others in the same way.

By withholding physical intimacy or using sex as a bargaining chip, they keep you off balance, always guessing, always seeking their approval. It's not just about depriving you of affection; it's about creating an environment where you feel inadequate, where you're constantly seeking validation. The lack of intimacy isn't just a punishment; it's a calculated move to make you feel powerless, to make you question yourself, and to reinforce their dominance in the relationship. They know how much you crave that closeness, and by withholding it, they keep you on edge, desperate for their approval.

And then, when narcissistic or toxic individual finally give in, when they finally offer that small glimmer of affection or intimacy, it feels like a reward—a fleeting moment that keeps you hooked. It's that small, intoxicating moment where you think things are going to be okay again, that maybe you're back in their good graces. But it's all an illusion. They're using these moments to sharpen their skills, to rehearse for their next victim, or to keep their side relationships thriving in the background.

This manipulation also serves another purpose: it keeps you so focused on trying to please them that you don't have the energy or clarity to notice what's really going on. The sudden withdrawal of affection, followed by moments of false reconciliation, creates a cycle of emotional highs and lows that keeps you trapped in their web. You become so consumed with trying to win back their affection that you don't notice the other signs—the late-night texts, the unexplained absences, the sudden changes in behavior. You're too busy trying to fix what's broken in the relationship to realize that they've already moved on emotionally or physically to someone else.

What's more, they weaponize your own insecurity against you. When you try to question them, when you bring up your concerns about the lack of intimacy or the changes in their behavior, they turn it back on you. Suddenly, you're the one who's being unreasonable, too needy, or paranoid. They might say things like, "You're imagining things," or "You're just trying to start a fight." This gaslighting (lying) makes you doubt your own feelings, and before you know it, you're apologizing for even bringing it up. It's a brilliant strategy because it keeps you second-guessing yourself while they continue to manipulate and deceive behind your back.

The truth is, when a narcissistic or toxic individual starts weaponizing their body in this way, it's a sign that the relationship has moved from a space of connection to one of manipulation and control. They're no longer invested in building something real with you—they're focused on getting what they need, whether that's validation, power, or the thrill of controlling someone else. And while you're left trying to figure out where things went wrong, they're already practicing their tactics for the next person, honing their ability to manipulate and deceive.

The cycle of withholding intimacy, offering small moments of affection, and then pulling back again is a form of emotional abuse. It's designed to keep you in a constant state of insecurity, to make you feel like you're not enough, and to keep you dependent on their approval. It's a tactic they use to maintain control, not just over you, but over the entire narrative of the relationship. And until you recognize it for what it is, you'll continue to be trapped in that cycle, always hoping for things to get better, but never realizing that they were never going to in the first place.

In a narcissistic or toxic relationship, this manifests as a pattern where the narcissist or toxic individual constantly shifts attention from one person to another. They may begin a relationship with intense focus on one person, idealizing them, only to suddenly turn their attention elsewhere once the relationship becomes too emotionally intimate.

This pattern is called "love-bombing and devaluation"—they idealize someone at first, making that person feel like the center of their world, but as soon as emotional closeness develops, they begin to devalue the person, withdrawing affection and seeking new supply elsewhere. This cycle ensures that the narcissist remains in control and never has to face the vulnerability that comes with true emotional connection.

Compartmentalization of Relationships

Narcissist or toxic individuals are highly skilled at compartmentalizing their relationships, keeping different aspects of their life separate so they can maintain control over various sources of supply. Each individual (supply) in their life serves a different purpose, whether it's providing emotional/ psychological support, admiration, conflict, or another form of attention. *For instance, they may have a partner who admires them, a friend who they manipulate into providing constant emotional/psychological labor, and a colleague they use as a rival to feed their competitive side. No single person can fulfill all these needs, which is why they rely on multiple sources of supply*. This is a critical point because these are the moments when narcissists or toxic individuals start to get sloppy, revealing cracks in their carefully constructed facade.

In my own experience, I had one such moment with BL that I'll never forget. We were having a conversation about an incident she claimed had happened with someone, and in the midst of recounting the story, she accidentally let the person's name slip. The moment the name left her lips, her entire demeanor shifted. Realizing her mistake, she immediately tried to backtrack. She insisted she never said the name, completely denying what had just happened, and then, almost as a defense mechanism, she shifted the blame onto me, saying I must have heard about it from somewhere else. She told me not to get upset, that it was in the past, and demanded that I not bring it up again.

This type of behavior is classic for someone who thrives on manipulation. Narcissistic or toxic individuals are masters at rewriting reality to suit their needs, especially when they feel their control slipping. The moment BL slipped up and revealed more than she intended, she shifted into damage control mode. She didn't just deny the slip-up; she manipulated the situation by preemptively scolding me for something I hadn't even reacted to yet. In doing so, she diverted attention away from her mistake and onto me, making me question my own reaction and emotions.

This tactic is what makes dealing with a narcissist so disorienting. They can make you doubt what you've just heard, what you've just seen, and even what you know to be true. In that brief moment of clarity where they expose a lie or a hidden truth, they quickly smother it with gaslighting, turning the situation on its head. You start to second-guess your own memory—did they actually say that, or am I just overthinking it? And that's exactly what they want. By confusing you, they regain control, making it harder for you to hold them accountable.

What makes these moments even more significant is that they offer a rare glimpse into the truth. Narcissists and toxic individuals are often so careful in crafting their narratives and controlling the flow of information that it can feel impossible to catch them in a lie. But when they do slip, it's telling. It shows that no matter how calculated they are, they cannot maintain the mask forever. However, the real danger comes in how quickly they can recover from these slip-ups, often turning the tables so fast that you find yourself apologizing for even noticing the inconsistency.

In my case with BL, that moment should have been a wake-up call, but her manipulation was so quick and so convincing that it wasn't until much later that I realized what had truly happened. At the time, I did exactly what she wanted—I let it go. I didn't press further or ask questions because, in the end, I was conditioned to believe that doing so would only lead to more conflict, more confusion, and more emotional exhaustion. And that's another layer of manipulation: they know that you've been worn down by constant mental and emotional strain, and they rely on your fatigue to keep their control intact. They make confrontation seem so daunting that you'd rather avoid it altogether.

Narcissists or toxic individuals often count on these slip-ups being forgotten or dismissed. They have an uncanny ability to make their victims feel like any questioning or challenging of their narrative is irrational or petty. And because they've usually spent so much time wearing down your confidence and your trust in your own judgment, you're often left feeling like maybe you're overreacting. This is how they tighten their grip, subtly reinforcing the idea that they are the rational one and you're the one causing unnecessary drama.

What's particularly striking about this moment with BL is how it reflects a deeper pattern in toxic relationships: the abuser's need to control the narrative at all costs. Once they feel like they've lost even a shred of control, they'll use any tactic available—denial, blame-shifting, emotional manipulation—to regain it. They might accuse you of being too sensitive, overreacting, or misinterpreting things. This keeps you off-balance, ensuring that they remain in control of the story. Even when they make mistakes, they've mastered the art of turning the situation around, making you question your reality, and ensuring their grip on the dynamic remains unbroken.

In these moments, it's crucial to remember that these slip-ups are not just accidents. They reveal the truth behind the facade, the manipulation, and the constant control. But it's also important to recognize that challenging these moments can feel overwhelming, especially after being subjected to years of psychological manipulation. Narcissists are skilled at making you feel powerless, at making you feel like confronting the truth will only lead to more pain. And that's what keeps so many people trapped in the cycle.

These small, seemingly insignificant moments where the mask slips are, in fact, windows into the reality of the situation. They remind you that, beneath the layers of manipulation, lies, and control, the narcissist or toxic individual is vulnerable to exposure. But it takes a strong sense of self—and often support from others—to see through their tactics and stand firm in your truth.

This compartmentalization also allows the narcissist or toxic individual to manipulate each relationship differently. They can show a caring, compassionate side to one person while being cold and distant with another. This selective behavior reinforces their control over others because it prevents people from seeing the whole picture. They can maintain their carefully crafted image with each individual while ensuring that no one person gets close enough to see the inconsistencies in their behavior.

When one supply begins to falter—perhaps a partner becomes disillusioned, or a friend grows weary of the manipulation—the narcissist or toxic individual has other relationships to fall back on.

They maintain a constant rotation of people to keep themselves emotionally and psychologically fed. This strategy not only serves their need for validation but also protects them from the emotional and psychological consequences of losing one source of supply. If one relationship deteriorates, they can quickly move on to another, leaving the discarded person (supply) behind without much thought or remorse.

A crucial point to consider is why narcissistic or toxic individuals often become extremely overprotective of their phone or laptop. This behavior might seem innocent at first glance, but in reality, it can be a major red flag. The question naturally arises: what are they hiding?

In relationships marked by manipulation and deceit, the need for secrecy becomes paramount to the narcissist or toxic individual control. Their phone or laptop is not just a tool for communication; it's a vault where they store evidence of their double life. Whether it's secret conversations, dating profiles, hidden social media accounts, or inappropriate relationships, they guard these devices like their lives depend on it. The thought of you discovering what's inside terrifies them because their entire narrative could unravel with just one look.

For the narcissist or toxic individual, control is everything. They control how you perceive them, how others perceive them, and even how you perceive yourself. Their phone or laptop is a vital part of this control. It's their personal hub for managing multiple personas—the charming partner, the victim, the supportive friend—all while concealing the truth. These devices may hold conversations with other romantic interests, derogatory comments about you to others, or even evidence of emotional and psychological or financial abuse. They know that if you were to discover these secrets, their web of lies would be exposed.

But more than just concealing evidence, the protective behavior around their devices is a form of psychological warfare. By keeping their phone or laptop out of reach, they create a sense of mystery, which fuels your insecurity and keeps you on edge. You might start to wonder what they're hiding or question your own suspicions, which is exactly what they want. This uncertainty leaves you in a constant state of anxiety, making you more vulnerable to their manipulation. The more you doubt yourself, the less likely you are to challenge them.

When you try to confront them about their protectiveness, they may respond with accusations, claiming you're being paranoid or invading their privacy. They'll twist the situation, making you feel guilty for even asking. In fact, they may go so far as to accuse you of being controlling or distrustful, flipping the script entirely. This tactic, often referred to as "projection," is a classic move in their playbook. They project their own dishonest and secretive behaviors onto you, making you the one who seems unreasonable or untrusting.

This protectiveness often comes with additional layers of manipulation. For instance, they might leave their phone or laptop in plain sight but locked with a password they refuse to share, further heightening the sense of secrecy. You might catch glimpses of messages or notifications, but never enough to piece together the whole story. This keeps you in a perpetual state of suspicion and unease, unsure whether to trust your instincts or give them the benefit of the doubt. It's a delicate balance they expertly maintain to keep you off-kilter.

Sometimes, the narcissist or toxic individual will take it a step further by planting seeds of doubt. They might hint that their phone contains work-related material, sensitive information, or personal matters unrelated to you. By doing so, they create a smokescreen, deflecting any suspicion back onto you. If you press further, they'll accuse you of violating their boundaries, flipping the situation into one where you feel ashamed for wanting transparency in the relationship.

At the heart of this overprotectiveness is their fear of exposure. Narcissist or toxic individuals are deeply afraid of being discovered for who they truly are. Their entire world is built on a foundation of lies, manipulation, and false narratives. Their phone or laptop holds the keys to this kingdom, and they know that once those doors are opened, it's all over. This fear of exposure is why they go to great lengths to protect these devices, even if it means damaging the relationship further by casting doubt and suspicion onto you.

It's important to recognize that this behavior is not just about secrecy—it's about control. By keeping their devices off-limits, they maintain a power dynamic that keeps you in the dark. They dictate what you can and cannot know, and in doing so, they assert dominance over the relationship. You're left feeling powerless, questioning your own sanity, and walking on eggshells to avoid triggering another argument over "trust issues."

In healthy relationships, transparency is key. There should be no reason to feel the need to hide your phone or laptop from your partner. Trust and open communication are the foundations of any strong relationship, and when these elements are missing—replaced instead by secrecy and defensiveness—it's a clear indication that something is deeply wrong.

When dealing with a narcissistic or toxic individual, it's important to trust your gut. If their overprotectiveness of their devices feels off, it probably is. This behavior is a telltale sign of deeper issues in the relationship—issues that they are desperately trying to hide. The sooner you recognize this for what it is, the better equipped you'll be to take steps toward protecting your own mental and emotional well-being.

Ultimately, the narcissist's or toxic person's phone or laptop isn't just a device—it's a symbol of their deception, their double life, and their need for control. It's the one place where they can hide the truth and maintain their grip on the narrative they've created. But the more they guard it, the more they reveal about their true intentions and the lengths they're willing to go to keep you in the dark.

Addiction to Power and Control

At the heart of a narcissistic or toxic relationship is the narcissist or toxic individual's desire for power and control. Control over others gives them a sense of dominance and superiority, which feeds their fragile ego. One person, no matter how devoted, can never fully satisfy this need for control. A single relationship would not provide enough opportunities for the narcissist or toxic individual to exercise their manipulative skills, nor would it offer the constant reinforcement of their superiority that they crave.

Narcissistic or toxic individuals often derive pleasure from manipulating people's emotions and creating drama. They thrive on the chaos they can cause and the emotional reactions they can provoke. This kind of manipulation provides a sense of power—proof that they are in control of the situation and the people involved. One supply may eventually grow wise to these tactics and become less reactive, prompting the narcissist or toxic individual to seek new individuals (supply) who will provide fresh emotional responses. The more people they can manipulate, the more powerful they feel.

Power dynamics also explain why narcissists often create conflict between their various sources of supply. By pitting people against each other—whether it's friends, family members, or romantic partners—they maintain control over everyone involved. They enjoy being at the center of conflict, as it reinforces their position as the one in charge. Each person is kept in a state of emotional turmoil, ensuring that the narcissist remains the focus of attention.

Exploiting Empathy and Generosity

A common tactic narcissists use is to exploit the empathy and generosity of their sources of supply.

People who are empathetic, caring, or naturally generous are often prime targets because they are more likely to give endlessly without demanding anything in return. However, no matter how much empathy or support one person offers, it's never enough for the narcissist. They will drain this person of their emotional energy, and when that well runs dry, they will seek out others who can provide a fresh source of emotional labor.

This exploitation of empathy creates a cycle of emotional exhaustion for the people involved. The narcissist demands more and more from their supply—more attention, more emotional support, more sacrifices—without ever reciprocating. Over time, the primary source of supply may become depleted, no longer able to meet the narcissist's endless demands. This is when the narcissist either begins to devalue that person or seeks out new individuals who can provide the emotional resources they need.

Narcissistic or toxic individuals are skilled at identifying people who are likely to give them what they need without question. They manipulate these individuals into believing that their love, support, or admiration is vital to the narcissist's well-being. Once the narcissist has extracted as much as they can, they move on to the next person, leaving the original source feeling drained and used. This process can repeat itself indefinitely, as the narcissist or toxic individual cycles through different sources of supply.

Fear of Rejection and Abandonment

Despite their outward bravado, narcissistic or toxic individuals are often deeply afraid of rejection and abandonment. The idea of being left alone is terrifying to them because it would force them to confront their own emotional emptiness. By maintaining multiple sources of supply, they ensure that they are never truly alone. If one person pulls away, they have others to fall back on. This safety net prevents them from having to experience the emotional and psychological pain of abandonment.

Reflecting on the divorce filing, it's clear why BL claimed to be unaware of the process despite her signature being on the paperwork. It wasn't that she was truly oblivious; rather, it was the realization that her security blanket was being pulled away from her that caused her to act as if she didn't know. For someone like BL, the marriage wasn't just a legal bond or a commitment—it was a source of security, power, and control. When that foundation began to crumble, she had to cling to whatever narrative she could to maintain her sense of control.

For BL, the marriage had always been about more than just a relationship; it was her safety net. It provided her with the emotional and financial stability she needed, along with a shield of respectability that she could wield when necessary. The thought of losing that security—of no longer having someone to lean on, manipulate, or blame—was terrifying for her. In her mind, the divorce was more than just the end of a relationship; it was the unraveling of the carefully constructed world she had built for herself. By denying her involvement or acting as though she had no idea what was happening, she was trying to regain control of a situation that was quickly slipping through her fingers.

This response is typical of a narcissist or toxic individual. When faced with losing their primary source of supply—whether that's emotional validation, financial support, or a constant target for their manipulation—they often react with denial, confusion, or an outright rewriting of reality. In BL's case, her refusal to acknowledge the divorce wasn't just a tactic to gain sympathy or stall the inevitable; it was her way of maintaining control in a situation where she felt powerless.

What's particularly striking about this behavior is how it underscores the narcissist's deep-seated fear of abandonment. For all their bravado and manipulation, at their core, narcissists are terrified of being left alone. They fear the loss of the person who props up their ego, caters to their needs, and acts as the steady supply of attention they crave. When the threat of abandonment becomes real—as it does in divorce—they'll go to great lengths to avoid it, even if that means feigning ignorance or playing the victim.

In BL's case, the denial of the divorce was not just an emotional reaction but a calculated move to retain her grip on the situation. By claiming she didn't know she was being divorced, she could paint herself as the wronged party—the spouse who was blindsided and betrayed. This narrative not only garnered her sympathy from those around her, but it also allowed her to perpetuate the idea that she was still in control. In her mind, as long as she didn't acknowledge the divorce, it wasn't really happening, and she could continue to manipulate the situation to her advantage.

This kind of denial can be incredibly frustrating for the other party involved. In my case, it felt like I was constantly walking through a maze of lies and half-truths, where nothing was ever straightforward. Every step toward ending the relationship was met with resistance, not just legally but emotionally and psychologically. BL's refusal to accept the reality of the divorce wasn't just about stalling the process—it was about keeping me emotionally and psychologically entangled in her web. By denying the truth, she forced me to constantly re-engage, to question myself, and to defend my actions, all of which kept her at the center of the narrative. – *You must keep telling yourself its not your fault and keep pressing forward.*

It's important to recognize that this kind of behavior isn't about love or attachment. BL wasn't resisting the divorce because she loved me or wanted to salvage the relationship. It was about control—about keeping her security intact and avoiding the vulnerability that comes with losing her primary source of narcissistic supply. For her, the marriage was a means to an end, and the thought of losing that safety net was too much to bear.

Her reaction also reveals a deeper truth about narcissistic or toxic relationships: the abuser often views their partner as an extension of themselves rather than an independent individual. In BL's mind, the divorce wasn't just a legal separation—it was the severing of a part of herself that she had used for years to maintain her identity and control. Losing that piece of herself was unthinkable, which is why she clung so desperately to the illusion that everything was fine, even when the paperwork said otherwise.

This kind of denial can be incredibly damaging, not just to the person being manipulated but to the manipulator as well. In BL's case, her refusal to acknowledge the divorce prevented her from facing the reality of the situation and ultimately prolonged the emotional pain for both of us. Instead of allowing the process to unfold naturally, she resisted every step of the way, making an already difficult situation even more painful and confusing.

BL's denial of the divorce filing wasn't about misunderstanding or ignorance. It was about fear—fear of losing control, fear of being abandoned, and fear of facing the reality of who she was without the security of the marriage to prop her up. For someone like BL, the divorce represented more than just the end of a relationship; it was the unraveling of her entire carefully constructed identity.

Their fear of abandonment also drives them to maintain control over their various sources of supply. By keeping people emotionally dependent on them—whether through manipulation, gaslighting, or creating a sense of obligation—they ensure that they are never without a source of validation. They play on the fears and insecurities of others to keep them from leaving, often creating an environment where people feel trapped or unable to escape the relationship.

The Cycle of Idealization, Devaluation, and Discard

The narcissist or toxic individual relationship cycle—idealization, devaluation, and discard—explains why one source of supply is never enough. In the idealization phase, the narcissist or toxic individual puts their new source of supply on a pedestal, showering them with attention and admiration. However, this phase is always temporary. Once the narcissist feels that they have "secured" their supply, they begin the devaluation phase, where they start to criticize, manipulate, and control the person. Finally, when the narcissist feels that they can no longer extract what they need from the relationship, they discard the person and move on to a new target.

This cycle is emotionally and psychologically devastating for the people involved, but it also explains why the narcissist or toxic individual is always seeking new sources of supply. No single person can survive this cycle indefinitely without becoming emotionally and psychologically drained. As soon as one source of supply begins to lose their usefulness—either by resisting the narcissist or toxic individual control or by no longer providing the desired emotional and psychological reactions—the narcissist or toxic individual begins searching for new people (supply) to idealize. This ensures that they always have a fresh source of admiration, attention, and emotional/psychological fuel.

One source of supply is never enough for a narcissist or toxic individual because of their unrelenting need for validation.

Flying Monkeys

The first time I encountered the term "Flying Monkeys" was while watching *The Wizard of Oz*, where the Wicked Witch sends her minions to do her bidding without question. Little did I know at the time, this concept would later hold real significance in my own life. "Flying Monkeys" refers to enablers—those people in a narcissist or toxic individual life who willingly or unknowingly help carry out their manipulative agendas. In my case, BL skillfully used her Flying Monkeys just like a carpenter wields tools, or perhaps more accurately, like a master chess player strategically moving pieces across the board. It was astonishing to witness how effortlessly she manipulated others, turning them into her unwitting pawns.

BL's Flying Monkeys weren't random; they were carefully chosen. She knew exactly which people to manipulate, how to play on their emotions, and how to present herself as the victim to ensure they would act on her behalf. It was almost like watching a masterful performance where she directed every scene, pulling strings behind the curtain, knowing exactly when and how to deploy her cast of enablers. They would carry out her wishes without question, doing everything from spreading lies about me to reinforcing her image as the poor, misunderstood victim who could do no wrong.

These enablers weren't just casual participants; they became an integral part of her game. BL used them to plant seeds of doubt in the minds of those closest to me—family, friends, even co-workers. She masterfully pitted people against each other, creating a web of deception so complex that it became difficult to separate the truth from the lies. Through them, she was able to maintain control, distorting the reality around me while isolating me from those who might have otherwise been a support system.

It's almost chilling how effectively BL moved her Flying Monkeys into place. Every interaction felt calculated, like a chess player thinking five steps ahead, positioning her pieces to ensure her victory. When she needed sympathy, they would offer it. When she needed someone to smear my reputation, they would do it. And when she needed validation for her false narratives, they were more than willing to back her up. The scary part is that most of these people had no idea they were being used. They believed her lies so completely that they became complicit in her manipulation without realizing they were just pieces in her larger game.

Watching it unfold was both bewildering and painful. I would often question myself, wondering how people I once trusted could so easily turn against me, how they could believe such outrageous fabrications without ever seeking the truth. But that's the genius of the narcissist's manipulation—they know how to play on emotions, how to exploit vulnerabilities, and how to frame their lies in a way that makes them seem believable, even sympathetic. BL was able to create this narrative where she was always the victim, and I was the villain, and her Flying Monkeys were more than happy to take on the role of protector.

What was even more baffling was how BL would position herself as the martyr, claiming to be the one who was misunderstood, unsupported, or mistreated. Her Flying Monkeys, enamored by her story and her ability to feign innocence, would rush to her defense, eager to help without ever questioning the truth of her claims. It was as if they saw her as some kind of helpless figure who needed their constant protection and support, when in reality, they were being manipulated into doing her dirty work.

These Flying Monkeys weren't just passive participants; they actively engaged in the smear campaigns, spreading rumors and half-truths, further isolating me while keeping her narrative intact. They became an extension of her power, carrying out tasks she couldn't openly do herself. It allowed BL to maintain a façade of innocence while they did the heavy lifting of dismantling my reputation and credibility.

Looking back, I realize how carefully orchestrated everything was. BL never made a move without calculating its impact, always staying several steps ahead. Just like a skilled chess player, she used each piece—each Flying Monkey—to advance her agenda while keeping herself removed from the direct conflict. She rarely got her hands dirty, yet she controlled every move.

And the worst part? BL's Flying Monkeys often believed they were doing the right thing. They thought they were helping someone who was in need, defending someone who had been wronged. They had no idea they were being played. BL fed them just enough information to get them on her side, never giving them the full picture, never letting them see the manipulation behind the scenes. And in their blind loyalty, they became complicit in her abuse, unwittingly furthering her destructive agenda.

The complexity of this dynamic is what makes it so hard to recognize, and even harder to break free from. When you're caught in the crossfire of a narcissist's Flying Monkeys, it feels like you're battling an entire army—not just the narcissist themselves. It's exhausting, demoralizing, and isolating. The more you try to defend yourself, the more they rally against you, convinced that you're the problem.

But what I've come to understand is that the narcissist's Flying Monkeys are just as much victims of manipulation as anyone else. They're pawns in a larger game, unable to see how they're being used to further the narcissist's control. They are so blinded by the narcissist's carefully crafted lies that they can't see the harm they're causing. In the end, they are just another tool in the narcissist's arsenal—one that is as disposable as any other once their usefulness runs out.

In reflecting on all this, it's astonishing how calculated and methodical narcissistic or toxic individuals like BL can be in moving their pieces, turning people against each other, and manipulating reality to suit their narrative. It's like watching a master craftsman at work—only instead of creating something beautiful, they're systematically tearing lives apart, piece by piece.

A narcissist's manipulation is so precise and deliberate, much like an artist chiseling away at a sculpture. The difference is that, in the hands of a toxic individual, the end result isn't something to admire; it's the dismantling of relationships, trust, and, often, the victim's sense of self. Every move is calculated, every interaction carefully staged to achieve their goals—control, validation, or simply to feed their insatiable ego.

The key takeaway here is this: don't blame the people who get caught up in the narcissist or toxic individual's web of deceit. They don't know what they're a part of. They are the unwitting extras in a carefully scripted production—a production where the narcissist is both the director and the star of the show. Just like in a movie, extras are hired to play their roles, often with no idea of the full storyline or the manipulations happening behind the scenes. These people—the so-called "Flying Monkeys"—are drawn into the narcissist's drama because they've been fed a narrative designed to cast the narcissist as the victim and the true victim as the villain.

In the process of healing, it's important to recognize this dynamic and, as hard as it may be, practice forgiveness. You have to forgive those people who were used as pawns in the narcissist's game, because they truly didn't know what they were doing. They were operating with the limited information they had been given, convinced that they were helping someone in need. The reality of the situation was far more complex than they could have imagined, but they didn't have the vantage point to see it.

Forgiveness becomes a vital part of the healing process because holding onto anger toward these enablers will only keep you stuck in the pain. Remember, they were just playing their part in a script they didn't write. They were manipulated just like you were, albeit in a different way. Their actions may have hurt you, but in many cases, they were acting out of misguided loyalty or concern, never fully understanding the truth.

"Forgive them, for they know not what they do," a powerful sentiment from the Bible, is particularly relevant in this situation. These people don't realize the extent of the damage they're contributing to, nor do they understand the full scope of the narcissist's manipulation. They're just there, caught up in a story that isn't theirs, playing roles they never asked for.

It's like watching a play where everyone thinks they're acting in a completely different genre. Some think it's a tragedy, some believe it's a comedy, but only the narcissist or toxic individual knows it's a psychological and emotional thriller where they're pulling all the strings. Everyone else is left confused, following cues that were carefully crafted to manipulate their emotions and actions. They're oblivious to the bigger picture, and in that sense, they are victims too—just in a different way.

By letting go of the resentment and forgiving those who were unknowingly complicit, you free yourself from carrying the weight of that hurt. Forgiveness doesn't mean you condone their actions or allow them back into your life without boundaries; it simply means you're releasing the hold that pain has on you. It's about reclaiming your emotional freedom and recognizing that the blame lies with the narcissist, not the people they manipulated.

In essence, part of your healing is not just understanding what happened, but also finding peace with those who were dragged into the chaos against their will. They didn't know the true nature of the narcissist, and often, they didn't see the manipulation for what it was. Their ignorance doesn't absolve them entirely, but it does help you realize that their actions were often misguided rather than malicious.

Forgiving them allows you to focus on your own growth and recovery, rather than staying trapped in the bitterness of what they did or didn't do. In time, you come to see that they were just as much a part of the narcissist's grand performance as you were and forgiving them is one of the most powerful steps you can take toward breaking free from the toxicity that once consumed your life... *Enablers just like monkeys flying are happy to be a part of something.*

5. Why Empowerment and Encouragement

Why did I choose to write about being the narcissistic or toxic individual's supply? The answer came through countless hours of research, watching videos, and reading stories from those who've experienced it firsthand. Many people, including self-diagnosed narcissists, offer "helpful" tips on how to heal or break free from the cycle of abuse, but that often leaves me asking one question: "Why?" Since when has the Devil ever spared someone shame in the process of controlling or defeating them? The irony is clear—the same people who have mastered the art of manipulation are now claiming to help others escape it. Can they truly show empathy, or is it just another form of control?

This concept mirrors much of what we see in society today. Look at individuals trying to change their lives after incarceration. They've "paid their debt to society," but re-entry is anything but smooth. Society, much like the narcissist, doesn't let them forget their mistakes. These individuals are constantly reminded of their failure, and the resources that should help them become productive members of society often seem just out of reach. Why is that? What kind of system perpetuates this endless cycle of shame and control?

Similarly, consider the victims of rape, especially those who must turn to law enforcement for help. Too often, they are met with indifference, a lack of empathy, and, worst of all, an insinuation that it was somehow their fault. This is not just a failure of the system; it's a reflection of a much larger societal issue. We need to take a long, hard look at ourselves and admit that change is long overdue. If we continue to ignore these issues, generations to come will suffer the same carnage.

Take a moment to reflect on those who work in public safety or public health. These are the fields that should provide comfort, yet how many of us feel truly safe in today's world? That sense of insecurity—doesn't it sound like the workings of a larger, almost cinematic narrative? In my next book, I'll delve deeper into this issue, exploring why we continue to feel unsafe even when surrounded by systems designed to protect us.

Everyone suffers in a narcissistic or toxic relationship—no one is exempt. This includes the narcissist or toxic individual themselves, whether they are male or female. It's what you could call "suffering in silence." Go ahead, laugh if you want, because silence is a favorite weapon of the narcissist or toxic individual. They use it to manipulate, to wound, to control. But here's the kicker—they can't handle the very tactics they so skillfully dish out.

As I mentioned in my first book, "Living in the Shadow: Understanding Narcissistic Supply," true healing is an inward process that works its way outward. The narcissist or toxic individual, however, believes the opposite—that control over their external world will bring them peace. But they're wrong.

Healing doesn't work in reverse, no matter how much they want to believe it. For those still trapped in these relationships, remember this: Find your strength. Your power. The narcissist or toxic individual may think they've got it all figured out, but they don't. They are just as lost in the chaos they create no matter how well they hide it. Healing is not about them. It's about you reclaiming your life from the wreckage and moving forward with the understanding that you are stronger than they ever imagined. The power is yours, not theirs.

Again, I need to emphasize the "WHY." Why did I choose to write about this? Because people need to know they're not alone. It's not just about recognizing the patterns of abuse, but also about shining a light on a particular group that is often silenced or ignored: fathers. I'm sounding the trumpet for those fathers who genuinely want to be present, who want to fulfill their role as fathers, but are blocked by the toxic narratives their partners create. These men are denied access to their children, their rights and emotions manipulated like chess pieces in a game they never agreed to play.

Fathers who want to be involved in their children's lives are painted as villains because they don't fit the story their partners have constructed. Imagine being a father who is trying to be there for your children, but every attempt is thwarted. The children are weaponized, turned against you, and you're made to feel like you're failing, even when you're doing everything right. Meanwhile, you're forced to pay exorbitant amounts of child support, not for neglecting your responsibilities, but because the system demands it—even when you've been there all along, doing what any father should do.

And then there's the children. They're told their father is a no-good, deadbeat who never cared for them. They grow up with a skewed perception, fed lies that were meant to maintain control, not to protect their emotional well-being. These children become collateral damage in a war they didn't start, and they carry those scars into adulthood. It's a cycle that feeds itself—a generational curse, if you will.

People need to know there's a way out, not just for themselves but for the children who are caught in the middle. Words have power, and we must use that power to break these cycles. It starts with looking at oneself, recognizing the role we play in either perpetuating or breaking free from toxic dynamics.

Narcissism and toxic behavior didn't start as the monster it eventually becomes. Like any process, it began somewhere small—a snide comment, an act of control disguised as care—and over time, it grew. It fed on insecurities, on vulnerabilities, until it became this massive force, capable of tearing lives apart.

But just as it grew, it can be undone. By recognizing these patterns, by giving a voice to those who've been silenced, by telling the truth about what's really happening behind closed doors. This is where healing starts. It starts with acknowledging that we are not alone, that these struggles are shared by many, and that we have the power to dismantle the lies, the manipulation, and the control. We can break free, and we can help others do the same.

In writing this, I'm not just speaking to those who are in the middle of a narcissistic or toxic relationship. I'm also speaking to the fathers out there, who are fighting for the chance to be in their children's lives, and to the children who've been led to believe a false narrative about their father. There is a way to reclaim your voice, your role, and your truth. Narcissism and toxic behavior thrive in the shadows, but once you bring it to light, it loses its power. This is how the healing begins—by naming it, confronting it, and taking steps to move beyond it.

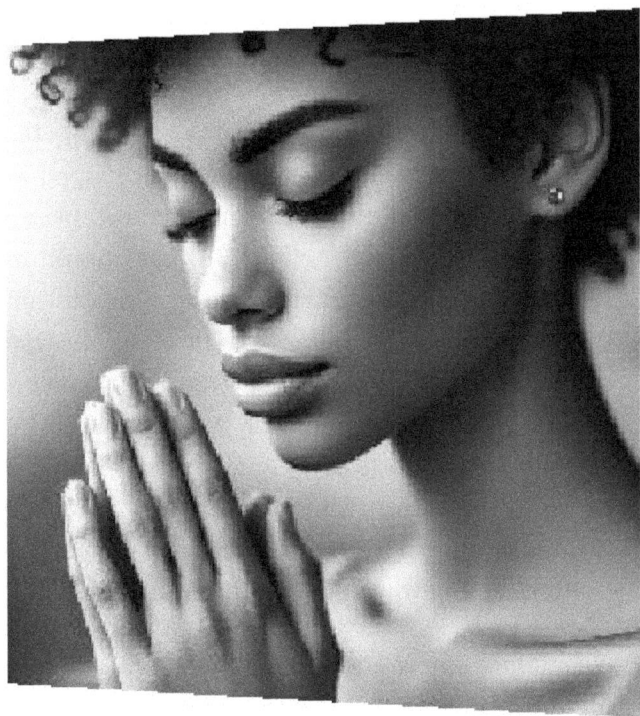

Epilogue

The truth, as it relates to me, is that I had forgotten something so powerful, something that shaped my entire life, that it bears repeating over and over in everything I write. Acts 2:38 has been my foundation—the one and only reason I've been able to step out of the shadow and confront all the trials and tribulations life throws my way. We often cling to cliches, phrases we think will give us strength, but in reality, they do little to stop the narcissistic or toxic individual from achieving their goal. Their aim is singular and strategic: to break you, to keep you from becoming who you are truly meant to be.

No amount of feel-good sayings can shield you from that. You must face the reality of what you're up against, and that reality begins with understanding yourself. Before you can hope to navigate the battlefield of a toxic relationship, you need to be aware of the weapons that narcissists wield—manipulation, deceit, emotional control—but even more importantly, you need to recognize your own worth and boundaries. Only by knowing yourself, by understanding your value, can you stand firm against these tactics.

"Understanding the Narcissist and Their Weapons" is only half the battle. The first and most important fight begins before there's any external conflict: it's the fight within yourself. If you can grasp that, if you can recognize the signs early and stand strong, you won't just survive—you'll thrive. You won't be caught in the web they spin, because you'll know what you're made of, and more importantly, you'll know that you never deserved to be in that situation to begin with. Knowing who you are and refusing to get entangled from the start is the key to reclaiming your power. ***Goodbye for now, see you in the next book.***

Milton Keynes UK
Ingram Content Group UK Ltd.
UKHW032039191024
449814UK00011B/642